Lynne Titchiner & Anne Winyard

Consumers' Rights

Arrow Books

Arrow Books Ltd
3 Fitzroy Square, London W1

An imprint of the Hutchinson Publishing Group

London Melbourne Sydney Auckland
Wellington Johannesburg and agencies
throughout the world

First published in Arrow Books Ltd 1975

Set in Intertype Times
Printed in Great Britain by The Anchor Press Ltd
and bound by Wm Brendon & Son Ltd
both of Tiptree, Essex

ISBN 0 09 911200 0

Citizens' Rights

General Editor: Frank Field, Director of the
Child Poverty Action Group and the Low Pay Unit

Much legislation has been designed to give ordinary people a
far better deal. But politicians and lawyers overlooked one
crucial fact. We don't all speak or understand their language.
Unlike the official handouts, this series is written by experts
whose work is to help people understand and claim their
rights. In other words it has been written with you in mind.
Each guide can be read without referring to any other material.
They each deal with all the main issues where you, the
citizen, find that 'they' are not telling you all you ought to
know.

Consumers' Rights

Lynne Titchiner and Anne Winyard

Lynne Titchiner was born in 1950. She studied Home
Economics at the North London Polytechnic and since then
has worked for the Camden Council of Social Service in the
Consumer Aid Centre in Kentish Town, London.

Anne Winyard was born in 1948. She studied at Oxford
University and has worked for two years in various Citizens'
Advice Bureaux in London run by the Camden Council of
Social Service, where she dealt with a wide variety of consumer
queries and problems. She is now training as a solicitor.

Acknowledgements

We should like to thank Cecilia Baker, John Bain, Fiona Beckett, Isobel Coleman, Frank Field, Professor Roy Goode and John and Olga Judson for all their invaluable help and comments on a first draft of the manuscript. Any errors or omissions which remain are entirely our responsibility. Our thanks also go to Paddy Field for her skilful and cheerful typing.

This book has been written so that it is not necessary for you to read it through from cover to cover. Throughout the text you will find signs like this ● referring you to other sections in the book. This is so that you can quickly find all the relevant information on a particular subject without having to refer to the list of contents.

This book went to press in July 1975 and information given is accurate to that date.

Contents

Acts of Parliament

This is an alphabetical list of the Acts and Regulations which are mentioned by name in the text. The page number against each Act refers to the place in the text where the details of that Act are explained. Of course several of the Acts, such as the Consumer Credit Act and the Sale of Goods Act, are mentioned more than once in the text.

1. Consumers and the Law

How often, when surveying the disintegrating remains of that pair of shoes bought two months ago, when sniffing cautiously at that fermenting yoghurt bought yesterday, when fingering the flabby folds of that pair of trousers that were smart, though admittedly dirty, before they went to the cleaners, have you thought vaguely 'there must be a law against this'?

This book is intended as a guide to the existing laws that affect our lives as shoppers and users of a variety of services such as cleaners, builders and garages. It also explains how to make sure that you avail yourself of the rights given by these laws to you, the consumer. The laws described are those of England and Wales. The laws of Scotland and Northern Ireland differ in a few minor details.

Spreading the word

Many consumer problems arise (or are made much harder to sort out) because so many consumers and traders don't really know what their rights and obligations are. There is obviously a need for far more consumer education which, if it is to be successful, must be available not only in schools and colleges but on the High Street, where it will reach every shopper and every trader.

Find out what services (if any) already exist in your own district. ●Getting some Help: page 128. Maybe the local Citizens' Advice Bureau deals with some consumer problems, or perhaps the local authority Trading Standards department gives general help and advice on consumer matters as well as doing their job of enforcing various laws and regulations. Some local authorities are providing consumer advisory services for residents in their area but they are still few and far between. If you would like to see a consumer advisory service or a consumer advice centre in your area contact your local councillor and ask what the council's plans are for providing this type of service. If the answer doesn't seem very satisfactory you may have to persuade the council that a consumer advisory service would be a good idea. Find out what services neighbouring local authorities provide, try and get hold of progress reports from some existing consumer advisory services or consumer advice centres and better still go and visit some if you can. Public opinion can go a long way in influencing a local authority as to how they spend their money – what about forming a pressure group?

Find out from the library if there is a consumer group in the area. If there isn't, you can start one either alone or with a few friends. The National Federation of Consumer Groups, ●page 134, will give you advice and the local paper will be interested in a new venture like this, which would help you to recruit members. With this book, we hope you will not only be able to help yourself, with your own problems, but help and advise others too.

The Law

There are two kinds of laws: criminal and civil. These laws are dealt with by different courts. Criminal law exists to protect the community as a whole, civil law to regulate people's dealings with each other. For example, murder, theft and dangerous driving are offences against the criminal laws, whereas civil laws cover such matters as marriage and divorce, wills and trusts, debts and contracts. Both criminal law and civil law consist partly of Acts of Parliament and partly of 'common law' – that is decisions made by judges on individual cases.

One of the most important distinctions between civil and criminal laws is that people such as policemen, factory inspectors and Trading Standards Officers are employed to make sure that the criminal law is not broken, and to prosecute anyone who does break it. A person found guilty of breaking the criminal law may be punished by fine or imprisonment. If however you feel that someone has harmed you by breach of the civil law, for example by slander or breach of contract, then it is up to you yourself to sue the offender. In other words the fact that an action is contrary to the civil law does not mean that the police or any other official body will step in and put a stop to it (with the exception of some breaches of the Consumer Credit Act, ●page 85, which aren't criminal offences but which will be the concern of the local Trading Standards Officer).

Civil Courts

County Courts deal with the smaller civil claims, including claims in contract for up to £1000 and Hire Purchase claims. Other civil matters go to the High Court. In some cases appeal can be made to the civil division of the Court of Appeal and thereafter to the House of Lords. Some civil matrimonial cases such as separation and maintenance orders are dealt with in the magistrates' courts.

Criminal Courts

Magistrates' courts are however mainly criminal courts. Anyone charged with breaking the criminal law must appear first in a magistrates' court. If the offence is too serious or the accused wishes to be tried by a jury, the case goes to the Crown Court. Thereafter appeal, if permitted, is made either to a divisional court of the High Court or the criminal division of the Court of Appeal and thereafter the House of Lords.

Striking the Bargain

When did you last make a contract? No need to cast your mind back to a distant afternoon in a solicitor's office signing copious documents – it was probably yesterday or even this morning. Every time you buy a pound of apples from the greengrocers, a bar of chocolate from a slot machine or take your shoes to the menders, you are making a contract. A contract is simply a legally binding agreement between two parties. It is quite possible to make a valid contract verbally, or indeed by putting a coin in a slot machine. Only certain more complicated kinds of contracts, for example HP and credit sale transactions and purchase and sale of houses, have to be in writing, or evidenced in writing.

Most contracts contain three basic elements:

(1) Offer (usually made by the buyer): 'I'll give you £13 for that coat.'

(2) Acceptance (usually made by the seller): 'Done.'

(3) Consideration (usually the promise to pay the price for the goods or services), in this case £13.

An offer can be withdrawn at any time until it is accepted. Once the offer has been accepted then a binding contract has been made and neither buyer nor seller can back out or alter the terms of the bargain without the agreement of the other.

When is the Contract made?

In many shops goods are displayed with prices marked on them. This, in law, is not an offer made by the shopkeeper, but is an 'invitation to treat'. In other words it is an invitation to the purchaser to make an offer to buy at the marked price. You make an offer when you point out the goods you want to the assistant. This offer is accepted when the assistant agrees to sell the goods at the stated price. The contract comes into existence when your offer is accepted. In self-service stores you make an offer at the check-out, which is accepted when the cashier rings up the sale.

Catalogues or advertisements produced by mail order

companies are 'invitations to treat'. Mail order companies accept offers made by customers when a letter of acceptance or the goods themselves are despatched (not when you receive the letter or the goods). This is because there is a special rule when buyer and seller are using the post to communicate with each other. Normally the acceptance of an offer is only effective when the person who made the offer has been told about its acceptance. Until then there is no contract. However when both sides are using the post, the acceptance becomes binding when it is posted.

An auction bid is accepted when the hammer falls.

Goods on Display

The moment at which the contract is made has practical consequences. It means that, contrary to popular belief, a shopkeeper cannot be compelled to sell goods which he has on display inside the shop or in the window, either at the marked price or at all. Only when the assistant has accepted your offer, and so made a binding contract, can you compel the shop to keep their side of the bargain and hand over the goods. There is no way in which you can by law force a shop to accept your offer. In other words you cannot force them to serve you. Similarly mail order companies do not have to accept your order (which is an 'offer'). They should of course promptly return any money sent.

Changing your Mind before you Buy

There is nothing to stop you backing out of a transaction *until* the moment that the shop actually accepts your offer, because until then there is no contract. You probably do this regularly in self-service stores by rejecting items from your basket before the cashier at the check-out rings up the sale. If you break something you will probably have to pay for it unless you can show that a breakage was virtually inevitable because, for example, goods were arranged so precariously on the shelves.

Changing your Mind after the Purchase

Once the contract has been made you have no legal right to demand your money back if you just change your mind about a purchase, or see the same article for sale elsewhere at a lower price. Only in certain circumstances, such as when goods prove to be defective, are not what you asked for, or are not what the seller said they were, have you the right to ask for, and receive, your money back. ●Your Rights: page 25.

Some shops, such as Marks & Spencers, are prepared for the sake of customer goodwill to refund money on faultless goods if you change your mind. Others, such as the John Lewis Partnership, refund the difference in price if you see the same goods for sale elsewhere at a lower price. In doing so they exceed their legal obligations.

However if a shop does display a notice saying that cash refunds will be given under certain circumstances (for example, money back if not satisfied) the terms of the notice form part of your contract with the shop and you can insist on a refund so long as you abide by any conditions stated, such as producing the receipt or returning the goods in their original packaging. Notices such as 'no refunds given: no goods credited or exchanged' do not necessarily form part of your contract with the shop and cannot be used by the shop to escape their legal obligation to compensate you if you buy faulty goods. ●More about this: page 26.

Contracts with the Manufacturer

We have seen that you always make a contract with the shop when you buy goods. In some instances you also make a direct contract with the manufacturer. One example is a *servicing contract* for a domestic appliance like a washing machine, which is usually made after the purchase of the appliance. Obviously the manufacturer is answerable if he does not carry out his contract properly. ●Servicing: page 57.

Sometimes new items carry a *manufacturer's guarantee* – in other words an agreement that the manufacturer will, under certain conditions, put defects right. A manufacturer's guarantee *cannot* limit your legal rights as a buyer to compensation from the shop if goods are faulty, so most guarantees are worth accepting and regarding as an extra safeguard. A manufacturer's guarantee can however, if you accept it, exclude the manufacturer's liability to compensate you for loss or damage caused by his negligence. ●Guarantees: page 34, ●Negligence: page 46.

Young People

A young person who is not yet eighteen is called a minor. Minors may have difficulty buying goods unless they pay with cash, and may find it hard to obtain credit facilities, such as bank overdrafts. This is because minors can only make legally binding contracts (which a trader could enforce to obtain payment) for goods which are 'necessaries'. This really means goods which the minor needs to maintain his usual standard of living, and so can include more than food and clothes. Expensive electronic equipment may be a 'necessary' for a young member of a successful pop group, but not for one of his less wealthy young fans. Shops usually safeguard themselves by insisting on cash.

Credit facilities may be difficult to obtain as a minor cannot be sued for repayment of money he has borrowed (for example, bank overdrafts), nor even can his adult guarantors.

Laws Protecting Consumers

Consumers are protected by both civil and criminal laws. The civil laws in the main govern the actual terms of the contract of sale made between buyer and seller. On the other hand the criminal ones lay down rules for retailers and manufacturers and provide criminal sanctions against offenders who do not follow the rules.

Civil Laws

It has already been explained that when goods are sold a contract is made between buyer and seller. Some civil laws provide safeguards for people taking out HP or credit sale agreements by laying down rules about the terms of the agreement (even down to the size of the print), about changing your mind and about repossession of the goods by the HP company. ●HP and Credit Sale: page 77.

Other civil laws protect the buyer by 'writing in' to every contract of sale certain implied terms about the quality of goods sold. If you are sold goods which are not of adequate quality, are not what you asked for, or are not what the retailer said they were, then the retailer has broken his contract and must put things right, for example by giving a refund. ●Your Rights: page 25. It is up to you to ensure that the retailer does so. In the last resort you can sue the retailer in the civil courts. ●Complaining: page 100.

Criminal Laws

The criminal laws in the consumer field seek to protect us all by providing criminal penalties (fine or imprisonment) for traders who, for example, seek to mislead the public by describing merchandise falsely or giving false price mark-downs, for traders who give short weight or short measure and for those who sell certain dangerous goods or appliances or potentially harmful foods. ●It's a Crime: page 88. Most of the criminal laws designed to protect consumers are enforced by Weights and Measures Officers, Trading Standards Officers or Public Health Inspectors, who are employed by local authorities. ●Who's Who: page 129.

2. Buying Goods

Your Rights

Every time you purchase goods you make a contract and
the law lays down certain terms that apply in every contract of sale. In brief, goods you buy

* must be as they are described ●details: page 27
* must be of merchantable quality ●details: page 27
* must be fit for their intended purpose ●details: page 29

and of course the seller must have a right to sell them.
●Details: page 40.

These are 'implied terms' of every contract of sale and
they are set out in the Sale of Goods Act 1893. If the goods
you buy do not measure up to these implied terms then the
seller has broken his contract with you and you will have a
claim against him. ●What Redress can you Expect?:
page 30.

Remember, under the contract of sale only the *buyer*
has these rights against the seller. If you are given a faulty
article as a present, you cannot claim against the seller under
the contract of sale, but the person who bought the article
can.

These rules only apply when you buy goods from someone selling in the course of a *business*. They don't all apply
when you buy from someone selling an article privately.
●Buying Privately: page 39. They do apply when you
'buy' goods in exchange for trading stamps.

These rules apply to secondhand goods and sale goods
as well - but a secondhand article or a 'second' cannot be

expected to have the quality or life-span of a new one and if a fault emerges it will, for that reason, be more difficult to prove that the seller has broken one of the implied terms of his contract. ●Buying secondhand: page 39, ●Sales: page 38.

Only sales of *goods* are covered by these rules, not sales of services. ●Services: page 50. Sometimes the difference is not so obvious. The test is: am I really paying for the skill and labour involved or for the actual goods? On this basis a contract to paint a portrait is *not* a sale of goods, whereas a contract to make a suit *is*.

Can these Rights be Taken Away from You?

No, they can't – so long as the sale was a 'consumer sale'. ●See below. Don't allow anyone to mislead you about this. Since the Supply of Goods (Implied Terms) Act 1973 came into force on 18 May 1973 your rights under the Sale of Goods Act *cannot* be taken away from you. Any exclusion clause (for example in a guarantee or an order form) or notice in the shop (for example, 'No refunds given') which tries to take away your rights under the Sale of Goods Act is *invalid* and you can ignore it.

Many shop staff haven't heard of the Sale of Goods Act or the Supply of Goods (Implied Terms) Act. You may have to explain their obligations to them.

A Consumer Sale

This is a sale to a private individual by someone who is selling in the course of business. Sales to people who are buying in the course of business (or who *say* they are, perhaps to get a trade discount) are not consumer sales, so exclusion clauses *can* operate. Also, the goods sold must be of a kind ordinarily bought by private individuals for their own use. A purchase at an auction is *not* a consumer sale.

What the Implied Terms mean in Practice

Goods must be as they are described

This is so whether by their own label, by the shop assistant or by you when you order. If you buy handkerchiefs described on their sealed box as blue, they must be blue not white. If you ask an assistant for a cotton tee shirt, she must not sell you one made of a synthetic fibre, unless you agree. Even in a self-service store, if you are relying on the label on a sealed container, the goods inside must correspond with the description given: 'pineapple rings' must be rings not chunks, 'sardines in olive oil' must not be sardines in tomato sauce. If you pick a jumper from a display stand marked 'woollen jumpers' it must be pure wool, not a mixture of wool and another fibre.

This overlaps with the Trade Descriptions Act 1968, which imposes criminal sanctions (fine or imprisonment) on retailers who describe their merchandise in a false or misleading way. A shop which sells courtelle jumpers as 'woollen jumpers' is in breach of the Sale of Goods Act and the Trade Descriptions Act. ●Trade Descriptions: page 94.

Goods must be of merchantable quality

Goods must be of a standard which a reasonable person, knowing of any defects, would be happy to accept for the price asked. Clearly for new goods this means without faults (except perhaps minor ones, such as a small scratch on the side of a cooker); for secondhand and sale goods it is not so easy to define. ●Buying secondhand: page 39, ●Sales: page 38.

The only exceptions are:

* faults which were specifically pointed out at the time of sale, and
* if you examined the goods before buying, faults which should then have been apparent.

If you buy a pair of walking shoes and the heel falls off within a week, then the shoes are obviously not of merchantable quality. Similarly, if your new automatic washing machine pumps water over the kitchen floor the first time you use it, or the new pyjamas you buy, which are sealed in a cellophane packet, turn out to have odd sleeves, neither can be said to be of merchantable quality.

However if the assistant says when you select a skirt, 'The hem is coming unstitched a little, but it's the only one we have left in your size', and you buy it, then you cannot go back later and ask for a refund because the hem is coming down. You made the contract knowing of the defect.

Either examine goods thoroughly before purchase, or not at all. If you only make a cursory examination you will have no claim for an obvious defect which a careful examination should have revealed. You would not be expected to notice a defect in the motor of a food mixer (in any case it may only become apparent later), but you would be expected to spot an obvious paint mark on the finish.

Now, what if the heel comes off the walking shoes after six weeks, or the automatic washing machine works fine for four months and then pumps water all over the floor? Were they of merchantable quality when you bought them? This really depends upon what caused the fault. If you have misused or neglected the goods, you cannot complain to the retailer. But if the fault which emerges was caused by an inherent (though hidden) defect present in the goods when you bought them, the situation is very different. If a reasonable person, knowing at the time of purchase of the inherent defect and its consequences, would refuse to accept the goods, then they are *not* of merchantable quality, and you *can* claim against the retailer.

It is obviously difficult for a layman to tell exactly what has caused a fault. However a common-sense line of reasoning is this: how long should an article of that type last without going wrong? If yours goes seriously wrong within that period and has not been misused, then the fault was probably caused by an inherent defect.

There are no easy rules on how long an article should last: a pair of sturdy walking shoes should, if you look after them, give many months of hard wear before developing any major faults. But it is quite unreasonable to suppose that a flimsier pair of 'fashion' shoes should last more than a few weeks if subjected to constant hard wear, perhaps in unsuitable weather conditions.

It would not seem unreasonable to hope for at least a year's service free from serious faults from a washing machine, a cooker or a fridge. The length of the manufacturer's guarantee (if any) will give you an idea of how long the manufacturers anticipate the goods will last without developing a serious fault.

Ultimately only the courts can decide whether an article is of merchantable quality.

Goods must be fit for their intended purpose

In many cases goods which are not of merchantable quality are not fit for their intended purpose either. For instance the walking shoes whose heel fell off are not of merchantable quality and neither are they fit for their intended purpose – walking.

On the other hand a new cooker which works perfectly, but has several bad scratches and dents on the oven door, is fit for its purpose (it works) but is not of merchantable quality (no one who had paid for a new cooker would be prepared to accept it).

This clause gives you added protection when you buy goods for some special purpose other than that for which they are normally used. If you want paint to waterproof your garden shed, then providing you state your requirements to the assistant, the paint he provides you with must be suitable for the purpose you specified. If he says he doesn't know whether the paint he has is suitable, but you still buy it, then you are not relying on his skill and judgment and you have no right to return the paint to him if it turns out to be unsuitable.

What Redress can you Expect?

Cancelling your contract – getting your money back

If you find the goods you have bought are not as described, are not of merchantable quality or are not fit for their intended purpose, then *act promptly*. If you want to cancel your contract (i.e. return the goods to the shop and have your money back), notify the shop *at once* – the goods themselves can be returned later.

If you delay once the fault becomes apparent you will lose your right to cancel and only be entitled to damages – that is, compensation for having bought a faulty article, for example a partial refund to cover the cost of repair and expenses incurred as a direct result of the fault. In the case of the automatic washing machine this includes such items as the costs of repairing the damaged floor and doing the washing at the launderette, or, in the case of a faulty new car, the costs of hiring a replacement or taking taxis where necessary.

If the article is satisfactory for a time and *then* develops a fault, it may be too late to cancel altogether and get your money back; you may have to accept damages instead.

If in doubt it's best to assume you're not too late and cancel your contract anyway; if you are in fact too late you can get damages instead. In the last resort only a court can decide whether you are in time to cancel altogether, but most claims don't get that far.

If you order goods which are delivered and are faulty, then you can't cancel immediately, but you should notify the shop and allow them a reasonable time to deliver a replacement. However if the delivery date was a condition of your contract, ●Delivery dates: page 37, you have a right to cancel if the replacement is not delivered in time to meet the original delivery date.

If goods are under a manufacturer's guarantee it is quite reasonable that, if you wish to, you should give the manufacturer an opportunity to put the defect right before cancelling your purchase with the shop. Notify the shop of the fault and explain that if the repair under guarantee is not satisfactory you will have no option but to cancel your contract. If the manufacturers can't or won't make a satisfactory repair, cancel your contract with the shop.

These two remedies

* cancellation plus damages or
* damages alone

are the only ones which a court can actually award and which you have a legal right to demand. In practice other remedies (such as replacement or repair) may be offered to you and can be just as satisfactory; but you can't insist on them since the seller is under no legal obligation to replace or repair. ●Complaining: page 100 – if the shop proves difficult.

Damages or Partial Refund

We have already said that unless you act *promptly* when you discover a fault you will lose your right to reject the goods and get all your money back – you will only be able to get damages (for example, a partial refund to cover the cost of the repair and incidental expenses). This may also be the case if an item has given a fair amount of service before the fault emerges, for example shoes which have given quite good wear but there is some indication that they have not given such good service as they should have done.

Another instance where a partial refund is sometimes offered, and is usually the most you can hope to get, is if you yourself are partly to blame, for example you buy a lined cotton dress with no washing instructions and take it to the launderette without finding out what method of washing/cleaning the shop recommends. The facings and linings shrink in the wash. The dress is still wearable but not as smart. The shop may admit they were partly to blame since no washing instructions were provided and offer you a small refund, letting you keep the dress. ●Complaining: page 100 – if the shop proves difficult.

Replacements

These are often perfectly acceptable, unless your need for the item has passed (for example if you bought it for a special occasion) or you have lost faith in the goods and/or the shop (for example if the shop twice replaces an item and each time it proves faulty, you will probably feel disinclined to accept a third replacement). If you don't want a replacement you are entitled to ask for your money back and/or compensation. ●Complaining: page 100 – if the shop proves difficult.

Repair

A repair free of charge by the shop (particularly for minor faults which may emerge some time after purchase) can also be quite acceptable. But if the shop offered to repair a new television that developed a serious fault during its first week of use, you would probably feel disinclined to accept a repaired TV instead of a new one. Again, if the implied terms of the Sale of Goods Act have been broken, you don't have to accept a repair but can insist on a refund and/or damages. ●Guarantees: page 34 – for repairs free of charge by manufacturer.

Credit Note

When you are offered a credit note you are either being offered *less* or *more* than you are legally entitled to.

If you decide you don't like the item you bought in a hurry in your lunch hour or that it doesn't fit, you have no legal right to cancel your contract with the shop and demand your money back (unless you specifically asked for this privilege at the time of purchase). If the shop offers you a credit note when you take the article back, they are exceeding their legal obligations and you are getting *more* than you are entitled to.

If, however, you buy an item which proves to be faulty, and when you claim your Sale of Goods Act right to reject it and get your money back you are only offered a credit note, then you are being offered *less* than you are legally entitled to. Never accept a credit note in these circumstances – keep the faulty goods and press the shop to give you a cash refund. *Once you have accepted a credit note* you have entered into a further agreement with the shop and *you cannot then insist on the credit note being exchanged for cash.* ●Complaining: page 100 – if the shop proves difficult.

Misleading Sales Talk

If someone makes a false statement about their goods (or services) they may be laying themselves open to legal action.

If the false statement was made by someone in the course of their business (for example by a shop, a travel agent or a garage) it may be a breach of the Trade Descriptions Act 1968 and the local Trading Standards department may be able to help. ●Trade Descriptions Act: page 94.

This might result in the trader being prosecuted, but does not automatically mean that you will be compensated. ●Compensation for you: page 99. However you may have grounds for action under the Misrepresentation Act 1967. Unlike most of the Acts which protect consumers this Act applies to transactions made between private individuals as well as transactions between a private individual and a business, such as a shop.

If someone makes a misrepresentation, i.e. an untrue statement which persuades you to enter into a contract (for example a purchase), the Misrepresentation Act gives you the right to cancel your contract, or at least get damages, if you show

* that the seller made an untrue statement of fact to you
* that he intended his untrue statement to persuade you to make the contract
* and that his untrue statement actually did persuade you to make the contract.

You don't have to show that his untrue statement was the *only* factor which persuaded you to make the contract. However, you will have no claim if *he* can show he honestly believed, on reasonable grounds, that his statement was true.

If you think you have grounds for a claim – act promptly. Otherwise you won't be able to cancel your contract, although you may still get damages. Notify the seller at once that you are cancelling your contract and explain why. If he refuses to return your money you can sue.
● Complaining: page 100.

Opinions (even if they are over-optimistic) such as 'marvellous bargain', 'the best on the market', are *not* statements of fact. Whereas phrases like 'six years old', 'it's done 15 000 miles', 'the service engineer fitted a new pilot light last month', 'we have overhauled and checked it thoroughly', *are* statements of fact.

In the case of a dispute it can sometimes be difficult to prove what was said. For this reason (particularly when buying from a private individual) it is a good idea to take someone else with you, who could act as a witness. Ideally any statements made by the seller should be in writing. If this isn't possible, get the seller to repeat his statement by, for example, asking 'How old did you say it was?' and make an accurate dated note of your conversation immediately afterwards.

Guarantees

Many manufacturers offer guarantees with their products, particularly electrical and mechanical products such as irons, washing machines, refrigerators, watches and cars. A guarantee is really an agreement that the manufacturer will put defects right, under certain conditions. A claim under a manufacturer's guarantee (particularly for domestic appliances) is often the quickest and simplest way of getting faults put right.

It is very important to remember that *no* guarantee given on or after 18 May 1973 can exclude your right to claim against the *shop* under the Sale of Goods Act. ●See also page 26. Guarantees given before that date could only exclude your Sale of Goods Act rights if the retailer was a party to the guarantee *and* you agreed the guarantee terms before purchase. (Garages often did this by incorporating the terms of the manufacturer's guarantee in their sales contract form which was signed by the garage and the purchaser.)

Guarantees are in two parts :

(1) *The manufacturer's promise*, for example 'We guarantee this appliance for a period of six months from the date of purchase against faulty workmanship or defective materials. Accordingly we undertake to repair or exchange *free of charge* any part found to be defective within the specified period.'

(2) *The conditions he imposes*, which you will have to stick to if you want to claim under the guarantee. They may include :

* 'For this guarantee to be effective the purchaser must complete and return the detachable half of this card within fourteen days of purchase.' You must do so if you want to be able to claim under the guarantee for repairs, etc.
* 'Faults resulting from misuse, neglect or accident are not covered by the guarantee.' This is fair enough.
* 'The customer is liable for any labour, postal or carriage charges.' This can greatly reduce the value of the guarantee to you.
* 'The manufacturer's decisions about alleged defects are final', i.e. they say that they alone can decide whether to

repair under guarantee. In fact a clause like this *cannot* stop you going to court if you feel they are unreasonably refusing to carry out the terms of the guarantee, but it will seldom be worth pursuing that far.

* 'This guarantee excludes all liability to compensate for loss or damage, however caused.' A clause like this means that you *personally* cannot claim against the manufacturer for loss or damage caused by his negligence. ●Negligence: page 46. If you want to preserve your right to claim damages for negligence then *don't* accept guarantees with such exclusion clauses (i.e. don't send back the guarantee card or actually claim for repairs under the guarantee). Some people cross out the clause and send the card back, but normally companies are not prepared to agree to any alteration in the conditions of the guarantee, and you can't make them.

Should you sign it?

So (apart from those which exclude liability for negligence) guarantees are *always* worth accepting, since they just provide an *extra* way of getting defects dealt with. If you decide to claim under a guarantee, you will normally be bound by its conditions, for example paying labour costs. There is nothing to stop you claiming your Sale of Goods Act rights against the shop instead (or as well, if the guarantee repairs are no good. ●Page 31.

Deposits

If you order or reserve goods and put down a deposit, then unless some contrary agreement is made, you are making a binding contract with the shop to buy the goods. It is possible – for example with prams and cots ordered before a baby is born – to make a special arrangement with the shop that under certain circumstances (such as a miscarriage) you can cancel your order without losing your deposit. If you want the goods by a certain date make this clear before you order, and make sure you can cancel your order without losing your deposit, if the goods don't arrive in time. Make sure any special arrangement for cancellation without loss of deposit is in writing, or its existence may be difficult to prove if you do want to cancel.

If you don't make any special arrangement and after ordering and paying a deposit you change your mind then you are breaking your contract with the shop and they have a right to retain your deposit.

Ordering Goods

Delivery Dates

It was explained in the previous section that if you want goods by a certain date, you should make this clear *before* you place your order, otherwise the delivery date will not be a term of your contract. Get the delivery date in writing, on the receipt if possible.

Even if you do not agree a definite delivery date with the shop when you order goods you cannot be expected to wait indefinitely. Unless, as is hardly likely, when you ordered the shop warned you of lengthy delivery dates and you agreed to wait as long as necessary. When you have waited a reasonable time (there are no easy rules on this – it might be several months, particularly if the goods have to come from abroad) then contact the shop. Warn them in writing that if they do not deliver the goods you have ordered within, say, another four weeks, you will cancel your contract and expect your deposit back. If the goods do not arrive within the time you stated and the shop have not offered any satisfactory explanation, you should write cancelling your contract and asking for the return of your deposit. If need be you can sue the shop. ●Suing: page 110.

Do not on any account, if you have ordered goods which take a long time coming, go and buy the goods somewhere else. You must notify the shop who accepted your original order of your intention to cancel your contract. Otherwise when the goods do arrive they have a legal right to assume you will stand by your original contract and will, if you refuse to accept the goods, have a right to retain your deposit.

Price Increases

If you order goods and the price goes up between order and delivery, can you be made to pay the difference? It all depends on what you agreed when you placed your order, since that was when you made your contract. In general it is assumed that when you make a contract to buy goods, you are agreeing to buy them at the *current* price. So if nothing is said (or written) about your having to pay the increased price, then you should only have to pay the price which the goods were selling for when you placed your order.

However, if the assistant explained you would have to pay any increase in price, or the order form or catalogue stated the current price but said for example 'subject to price fluctuations', then you will have to pay the increased price.

It is a good idea to get a copy of your order form and a receipt for any deposit paid.

Sales

When you buy goods in sales you still have your Sale of Goods Act rights. ●Your Rights: page 25. Remember you can't complain about faults which were specifically pointed out to you before purchase and that if you examine goods before purchase you can't claim for faults you should have noticed.

No reasonable person expects high quality from sale goods marked 'shop soiled', 'imperfect', 'seconds' or 'substandard', so if a fault emerges it will be difficult to rely on the 'merchantable quality' rule. You would however have a claim against the shop if the goods were completely useless.

On the other hand many shops, in their sales, sell their

ordinary stock at somewhat reduced prices. In this case, so long as the goods are not being sold as 'seconds', 'imperfect', etc., you are quite entitled to expect the goods to be of the same quality as full price goods.

Remember notices like 'no refunds on sale goods' *cannot* take away your Sale of Goods Act rights if the goods should prove faulty. ●Can these Rights be Taken Away From you? : page 26.

Buying secondhand

Purchases from private individuals are discussed separately. ●Buying privately: page 39.

Secondhand purchases from dealers are covered by the Sale of Goods Act. ●Your Rights: page 25. Furthermore you should not be given misleading information about the goods. ●Misleading Sales Talk: page 33.

However, if a secondhand item goes wrong it will be much more difficult to succeed in a Sale of Goods Act claim against the dealer than it would in the case of a new item. No reasonable person expects a secondhand item to perform or appear as it did when new, nor to last as long without needing repair. A secondhand item is of 'merchantable quality' if it performs as well as items of that age normally do, bearing in mind the amount of use it has had and the price paid. If this sounds vague, it *is*; that's why claims are difficult.

If in doubt try and get the goods inspected by someone with specialist knowledge, ●see remarks in Buying Privately: page 39.

Some retailers give guarantees on secondhand items. They are normally worth having, even though they are (obviously) for a shorter period than the original manufacturer's guarantee. ●Guarantees: page 34.

Buying Privately

When you buy goods from an individual selling privately you have *no* Sale of Goods Act rights as to their quality or fitness for purpose, though the goods must fit their description and the seller must have a right to sell them. ●Your Rights: page 25. You also have rights under the Misrepresentation Act 1967. ●Misleading Sales Talk: page 33.

However, taking legal action against a private individual can be a perilous business. He may disappear, leaving no forwarding address, or turn out to have no money. It is much better to miss the chance of a possible bargain than buy an expensive white elephant.

If you don't know much about the type of goods you are buying then try and get someone who does have some specialist knowledge to inspect them for you, for example the AA for secondhand cars. Don't be embarrassed about examining the item really thoroughly or getting someone else to do it for you. So long as you take reasonable care the seller should have no objection – unless he has something to hide.

Be on your guard against some less scrupulous dealers who masquerade as private individuals. Watch out for recurring advertisements or car advertisements where the advertiser doesn't have the car he advertised but happens to have a different one or to have a friend who has another. The advertising manager of the paper in which the advertisement appeared may well be able to advise, since often he makes these dealers pay trade rates for their 'private' advertisements.

Buying Goods which aren't the Seller's Property

Stolen Goods

If you buy stolen goods innocently, you are not committing any criminal offence but you can normally be made to give the goods back to their rightful owner. If this happens your only remedy is to sue the person who sold you the goods, who will probably have disappeared. 'Market overt' is an exception to this rule.

Goods on Hire Purchase

Goods bought from someone who has no right to sell them (for example someone who has them on an HP agreement) cannot in general become the property of the buyer. However if you buy a motor vehicle without knowing it is on HP, then you become its rightful owner. This only applies to motor vehicles, not other goods on HP.

If you suspect that the car you want to buy might be the subject of an HP agreement you can ask your local Citizens' Advice Bureau, ●page 128, to check for you by letter or by telephone, from HP Information Ltd. This non-profit-making organization keeps records of ownership of vehicles bought on HP agreements. They will not deal with inquiries from private individuals. More details about HP ●page 75.

'Market Overt' (or open market)

If you buy goods 'in market overt' you become the rightful owner, even if the goods were stolen or the seller had no right to sell them. A purchase from any shop within the City of London, or on market day from any English market established by Parliament, royal charter or local custom is made 'in market overt'.

Doorstep Salesmen

Not all doorstep salesmen are crooks. Many reputable firms use this method of selling. Some of them have formed an association known as the Direct Sales and Service Association which lays down a code of conduct for its members. The Association produces a leaflet called *Facts you should know about Buying at Home.* ●Trade Associations: page 138. If the good are faulty, you have the same rights as for shop purchases. ●Your Rights: page 25.

Unfortunately there are still some less reputable firms whose main objective is to make an immediate sale at a high price, often with no after-sales service. Salesmen may try to mislead prospective buyers in order to gain entry to the house. The salesman may for example pretend he works for a 'research organization' doing a survey on food prices. Once indoors he tries to sell a freezer and a supply of inferior quality frozen foods at an inflated price, all on 'easy terms' (normally easier for the seller than the buyer).

If a doorstep salesman calls, remember:

* Ask to see his credentials
* Don't sign any agreement until you have had time to think it over, and if in doubt seek advice. ●Who's Who: page 128.
* Hire purchase and credit sale agreements signed 'off trade premises', i.e. in your own home, can be cancelled if you act promptly. ●Changing your Mind: page 80.
* Watch out for ordinary *hire* agreements (not hire purchase). You could be agreeing to pay several times over for an item you will never own.
* Watch out also for personal loan agreements. ●Types of Credit: page 75. You will have no right to cancel and must continue paying even if the goods go wrong.

Mail Order

Most mail order firms either sell through catalogues or through advertisements in the press. People buying goods by mail order have the same Sale of Goods Act rights as for shop purchases. ●Your Rights: page 25.

Safeguards

* Only deal with reputable and well established firms who give 'money back if not satisfied' guarantees or allow you to have goods 'on approval'.
* If you order from a press advertisement keep the magazine or newspaper containing the advertisement.
* Never send cash with an order, only postal or money orders, cheques, etc. Keep the counterfoils.
* Make sure to put 'not examined' if you have to sign for

the goods when they arrive, and you don't have a chance to inspect them properly.

* When returning goods, pack them carefully and always get a certificate of posting from the GPO. Enclose a note saying who they are from, and write separately (recorded delivery) saying why you are returning the goods and requesting a refund. If there is an order number, agency number or despatch number, remember to quote it.

Complaints

In the first instance take complaints up with the mail order company. If you get nowhere and you bought through a press advertisement, it is worth taking the complaint up with the advertising manager of the publication in which the advertisement appeared. The Advertising Standards Authority, ●page 139, may also be able to help. Most newspapers and periodicals now operate a scheme to compensate readers who have sent money in advance to a mail order company which goes bankrupt. If stuck get advice. ●Who's Who: page 128.

If You Want to Change your Mind

Your right to change your mind depends upon when the contract of sale is made. ●When is the Contract made? : page 20. You are only making an offer when you despatch your order to the company. The company does not have to accept your offer, but they should of course promptly return any money you sent. The actual contract is made (and becomes binding) when the company accept your offer by despatching the goods or sending you a letter of acceptance.

You have a right to withdraw your offer so long as you let the company know *before* they accept it. Send a letter withdrawing your offer by recorded delivery.

If you buy through an agent (perhaps one of your neighbours), your contract with the mail order company is made when the agent accepts your order.

Unsolicited Goods

If you receive goods through the post which you have not ordered, you do not have to pay for them or send them back. Neither can you treat them at once as a free gift, nor throw them away. You can either

* *do nothing* and just keep the goods safe for six months; within that period allowing the sender to collect them if he wishes. If he fails to do so, the goods become yours.

or

* *write to the sender* giving your name and address and saying that the goods are unsolicited. The sender then has thirty days in which to collect the goods. If he fails to do so, the goods become yours.

If the sender demands payment or threatens legal proceedings he can be fined under the Unsolicited Goods and Services Act 1971. Contact your local Trading Standards Officer. ●Who's Who: page 129. In some cases he may refer you to the police.

Auctions

At an auction sale goods are sold to the highest bidder, normally for cash. The general rules about making contracts apply to auction sales. ●Striking the Bargain: page 19, as well as some special rules outlined below.

The 'Conditions of Sale'

'Conditions of sale' (for example that goods purchased must be removed from the auction rooms within twenty-four hours; or that the auctioneer accepts no responsibility for mistakes in the catalogue) must be displayed in the sale room or printed in the catalogue.

Bidding

The auctioneer normally starts his sale of each item (called a 'lot') by requesting bids. Legally, this is not an offer to sell but (like goods on display in a shop window) is an invitation to prospective buyers to make offers, i.e. bids. The prospective buyer makes a bid by giving a sign to the auctioneer or by calling out the price he wants to offer. The bids gradually get higher and finally all bidders except one drop out. The auctioneer (who is the seller's agent) doesn't *have* to accept this last and highest bid, but he nearly always does, unless the seller put a reserve (i.e. minimum) price on the lot and that price hasn't been reached. The lot is 'knocked down', i.e. sold to the highest bidder, when the auctioneer's hammer falls.

Faulty Goods

If you intend to bid for a lot at an auction you *must* inspect the goods carefully beforehand. Goods sold at auctions are often secondhand and it is up to the buyer to discover any faults. Articles marked 'a.f.' ('at fault 'or 'as found') in the catalogue will definitely have some faults. The Supply of Goods (Implied Terms) Act does not apply to auctions, ●A Consumer Sale: page 26, so it is possible for your Sale of Goods Act rights to be excluded, for example by notices in the sale room or catalogue like 'all express and implied conditions and warranties, statutory or otherwise, are hereby excluded'. If you are persuaded to bid by false statements made about a 'lot' by the auctioneer or the seller you are entitled to refuse to pay for the lot or return it and demand a refund.

3. Negligence

Claiming against the Manufacturer for Faulty Goods

We have seen in the previous chapter that if you buy faulty goods you can in general look to the shop for redress .There is no implication that the shop is to *blame* for the defect in the goods, merely that the implied conditions of the contract of sale make the shop legally responsible for compensating the purchaser.

What if the goods harm someone apart from the purchaser? Take for example an electric toaster, given as a wedding present, which because of a fault in its internal wiring gives a severe electric shock to one of its new owners. He has no contract with the shop where the toaster was bought and so cannot claim damages against the shop for breach of contract and loss of earnings resulting from the injury. In these circumstances it is possible to claim damages against the manufacturer for negligence if you can show three things:

(1) that the manufacturer had a *duty of reasonable care* towards you

(2) that he *failed* in this duty, and

(3) that his failure resulted in *damage* or injury which he should *reasonably have foreseen.*

In other words the manufacturer's liability for negligence is based on *fault*, whereas the shop's Sale of Goods Act liability is not.

Proving Negligence

Let us take these points in turn.

Duty of reasonable care

This is simple – any manufacturer has a duty to take reasonable care in making his products. The law does not require him to ensure all his products are perfect, but does require him to take all reasonable steps to ensure that his products have no potentially dangerous or harmful faults. He owes this duty not only to the purchaser of his products but to anyone likely to be harmed by his failure to exercise reasonable care in manufacture, such as the user of the toaster.

Failure to take reasonable care

This may be more difficult to establish. It is up to the injured person to prove that the fault which injured him or damaged his property actually resulted from the manufacturer's failure to take reasonable care while making the product (rather than mishandling or faulty storage after the product left the factory). The existence of faulty wiring inside a new toaster is, however, a strong indication that the manufacturer was negligent. It would be a defence for the manufacturer to prove that the wiring had been tampered with after the toaster left the factory (a defence which can't easily be used with ready-packaged goods) but no defence to prove that he had produced many thousands of apparently faultless toasters in the last year.

Foreseeable damage

A negligent manufacturer can only be held liable for damage which he should reasonably have foreseen. Any car manufacturer could be expected to foresee that a car with a faulty brake cable might cause a road accident, damage to other vehicles, and perhaps to property, injury to the driver, passengers and other road users. The injuries might result in loss of earnings and the owners of the damaged vehicles may need to hire replacements while repairs are done. The victims could include all these expenses in their claims against the negligent manufacturer. The manufacturer could not reasonably be expected to foresee that one of the injured pedestrians was on his way to place a bet on the afternoon's race and missed a win on a 50–1 outsider as a result of the accident – the pedestrian could not include a loss like this in his claim.

Exemption Clauses (Manufacturers)

Any agreement you make with the manufacturer (such as a manufacturer's guarantee if you accept it) can, if it is clearly worded, exclude the manufacturer's liability to compensate you for loss or damage caused by his negligence. This exclusion only applies to the person who actually makes the contract with the manufacturer, e.g. fills out the guarantee forms, and cannot prevent anyone *else* claiming damages for negligence. If you want to maintain your right to claim damages for negligence you should not accept guarantees with such exemption clauses. Look out for words like 'This guarantee excludes all liability to compensate for damage or loss, howsoever caused'.

You can try crossing out the clause before signing and returning the guarantee form. If you only have to complete and return a registration card then write a covering letter. Always keep copies. The manufacturer may however not be willing to accept your amended version of the guarantee and you can't compel them. ●Guarantees: page 34.

If you feel you have a good case against the manufacturer, apart from an exemption clause in the guarantee, it's probably worth getting legal advice on whether the clause is in fact well enough worded to protect the manufacturer.

Claiming against the Shop too

If the person who bought the defective article is the one who suffers injury or damage from the defect then he probably has, as well as a claim against the manufacturer for negligence, a claim against the shop under the Sale of

Goods Act for breach of the implied terms of the contract of sale. ●Your Rights: page 25.

Alternatively it is sometimes possible to claim against the shop for negligence, whether or not you actually bought the defective article. If in the case of the faulty toaster the manufacturer had in fact, prior to the date of sale, told the shop to withdraw that line of toasters from sale and return them to the factory for a safety check (or other customers had complained of electric shocks) but the shop had continued to sell the toasters, then the injured person would probably have a claim for negligence against the shop.

When you have grounds for claiming against both manufacturer and retailer you should notify both of them as soon as the defect is apparent. There is nothing to stop you claiming against both of them – though you cannot be paid double damages for the same misfortune. If both are found negligent then in practice each will have to pay you according to their degree of blame. If the shop is found to be in breach of the implied conditions of the contract of sale then the retailer will have to compensate you for his breach of contract in addition to any damages the manufacturer may have to pay for negligence.

4. Services

This chapter is in two parts. The first part explains the general legal rules which apply when you buy a service. The second part gives some details about particular services.

When you buy a service, such as dry cleaning, electrical or mechanical repairs, building work, or transport, you make a contract with the person who supplies the service. Often the contract is verbal, not written.

Usually you expressly agree some of the terms, for example 'cleaning and retexturing', 'relining the clutch', 'shampoo and set'. If nothing specific is agreed about other matters such as the standard of workmanship, the materials and the care that will be taken of your possessions, the firm is obliged to perform the service in a reasonably competent way, to use materials that are reasonably suitable for the job, and to take reasonable care of your possessions ●What Standard of Work Can You Expect? : page 55. In practice you will often find firms use standard form contracts which take away some of your rights. ●Exemption Clauses: page 51.

Remember too that a firm which describes the services it offers in a false or misleading way may be guilty of a criminal offence, and if prosecuted and convicted, could be ordered to pay you compensation. ●Trade Descriptions: page 94.

Looking after Other People's Possessions
When you agree to look after your friend's record player

while she is away, you have a duty to take care of it, even though you are not being paid for your pains. Equally, the cleaners, the cobblers, the warehouse, the cloakroom attendant and the garage have a duty to take care of your possessions left temporarily in their charge, unless other terms are agreed. ●Exemption Clauses: see below. If your possessions are damaged, destroyed or lost while in their care, they will be liable *unless* they can show they took all reasonable care to prevent the mishap. In practice, cleaners, repairers, storage firms and so on will find this difficult to prove unless the mishap was caused for example by fire (despite adequate fire precautions) or theft (despite adequate security locks and burglar alarms).

Exemption Clauses (Services)

Exemption clauses are very popular with suppliers of services. A properly worded exemption clause in a contract to supply services can absolve the firm providing the service from *all* liability for any mishap (including death or complete destruction of your property) even if the mishap is obviously their fault. This is quite different from contracts for the sale of goods, where *no* exemption clause can exclude your Sale of Goods Act rights.

Look out for:

* 'We accept no responsibility for any claims or demands whatsoever by whomsoever made for any damage to or loss of personal property, whilst in our care.'
* 'Sunnydays Holidays do not under any circumstances accept responsibility for loss of life, personal injury, illness or loss or damage to baggage or personal effects, howsoever caused.'
* 'All work is undertaken at the customer's risk.'

If the firm supplying the service is going to rely on an exemption clause like the three above, the clause must be part of the contract.

In other words you must have been given notice of the clause – perhaps in the small print of a form you signed, in a poster displayed on the wall or the 'conditions' on the back of a ticket – *before* or *at the time* you made the contract. An exemption clause *won't* protect the firm if they give you notice of it *after* you made the contract: for example an exemption clause on the wall of a hotel bedroom, rather than in the entrance hall where the booking (i.e. the contract) was made, will *not* protect the proprietors unless the guest stayed regularly at the hotel, so was well aware of the contents of the clause. The Court of Appeal recently decided that conditions printed on a ticket issued by an automatic machine at the entrance to a multi-storey car park were given *too late* and could not be relied on by the garage owners.

Furthermore the clause must be clearly worded if it is to exclude liability for any mishap caused by negligence (i.e. carelessness). Look out for the words 'howsoever caused' as they will normally do the trick. If one of the firm's employees misled you about the meaning of the exemption clause, or agreed to take particular care of your goods despite the clause, a court might decide the clause didn't apply.

In practice, read any forms carefully before you sign. If you don't have to sign anything look out for notices displayed or conditions on the back of tickets. You can try to get the firm to cross out the exemption clause or try to find another firm which doesn't insist on having exemption clauses in their contracts. If you don't succeed and you want to use the service your only way of protecting yourself is to get insurance cover.

When Work is Sub-contracted Out

A firm which sub-contracts work out *without* your knowledge or permission (for example work sent to a specialist firm, goods in storage sent to another company's warehouse) is liable if your possessions are lost or damaged when in the sub-contractor's care – and *cannot* rely on any exemption clauses to escape liability.

To cover themselves, many firms now put on tickets or notices phrases like 'we reserve the right to sub-contract work out, wholly or in part', so you will not be able to claim they did so without your knowledge or permission. In this case you may be able to claim against the sub-contractors if your goods are lost or damaged.

In either case it may be quite a struggle to get compensation. ●When Things go Wrong: page 56.

How Much do You have to Pay?

If you *don't* agree a price before the work is done you are only bound to pay a reasonable price. This means no more than most reasonable local firms would charge. For example, if you had a lock changed on your front door and you were sent a bill for £25 which you thought seemed rather a lot, you should phone round and ask a number of other locksmiths what they would charge for the same job, then pay the average price. You would not be entitled to do this if you were paying the extra amount for something special, like a two-hour service, unless the company claimed to charge no more for it.

It is normally more sensible to agree a price in advance ●Estimates: see below. If a price list is displayed in a reasonably obvious place, such as in the window of the hairdressers or on the wall of the laundry or dry cleaners, you are assumed to have agreed the price in advance and you are not entitled to query the bill or refuse to pay even if you didn't notice the list.

Estimates

With many jobs, for example repairs of electrical or mechanical goods (TVs, cars), or building and contracting work (plumbing, re-wiring, putting in central heating), it is almost impossible for the layman to tell what needs doing and to gauge a reasonable price. For this reason it is a good idea to get several estimates.

When comparing estimates, make sure they are for similar work, for example supplying a comparable amount of materials or replacing a comparable number of parts. Normally estimates are free, but check this in advance.

Once you have agreed on an estimate you have made a legally binding contract: you can't decide later only to pay what you consider a reasonable price. When you accept a written estimate make sure you read the small print. In general a firm cannot charge you more than was agreed upon, unless there are clauses in the accepted estimate such as 'prices quoted are subject to fluctuation' or 'prices quoted are applicable for one month from date of estimate'.

One objection to estimates is that a firm may sometimes give a high estimate, particularly if they are not sure quite how much work the job will involve. If you accept the estimate you will be bound to pay the high figure even if the job turns out to be a fairly simple and inexpensive one. You minimize the risk of this happening by getting several estimates.

Time Limits

So long as you state clearly that work must be finished by a particular date, and the firm agrees, that time limit is a term of your contract. When large companies negotiate commercial contracts they often include 'agreed damages' clauses – the firm doing the work must pay so much for each day they run over schedule. Try if you can to include a clause like this in your contract. Otherwise you can claim compensation from the firm.

For example if you are having a suit or a dress made for a special occasion and the tailor does not have it ready in time, you would certainly be entitled to deduct from your final bill the cost of hiring a replacement. If it was a 'once only' outfit, like a wedding dress, you would be entitled to refuse to pay for it altogether, and claim reimbursement for any additional expense, like the extra cost of buying a substitute.

What Standard of Work Can You Expect?

We've already seen that, unless a different agreement has been reached, you can expect work to be of a reasonable standard and the materials used, such as spare parts, paint, building materials, to be reasonably suitable for their job.

A reasonable standard means a standard which a competent member of that trade or profession would consider adequate. It is reasonable to expect a higher standard of workmanship from a man calling himself a skilled carpenter than from the odd job man who normally cleans your windows but on occasion agrees to do 'a bit of woodwork' for you.

In practice it can be very difficult for a layman to judge what a 'reasonable standard' is. It is normally fairly obvious if the work is quite hopeless – the roof leaks as much as it ever did, the vacuum cleaner still doesn't pick up the dirt, the radio continues to crackle infuriatingly – but sometimes the work, though not totally useless, isn't as good as you had hoped. Sometimes you have a suspicion that although the original fault has been dealt with, another has emerged. You wonder whether the firm should have taken so long (and charged so much) to locate and cure the fault. You wonder whether it was really necessary to fit a new valve. The answers to all these questions depend upon what a competent firm in that line of business would have done.

Some trade associations will help sort out disputes about services between customers and their member firms, for example the Motor Agents Association (for garage repairs) and the Association of British Launderers and Dry Cleaners. ●Trade Associations: page 135.

Choosing the Firm

Remember that membership of trade associations is not

compulsory so not all firms belong. It is often a good idea to choose a firm which *does* belong; ask the firm or get a list from the appropriate trade association.

It is also sensible, before asking a particular firm to do work for you, to inquire about them locally from friends, neighbours, a local consumer group or Consumer Advice Centre. ●Who's Who: page 128.

When Things go Wrong

First complain to the firm. ●Complaining: page 100. If this doesn't work you can try appealing to the relevant trade association if there is one and the firm is a member. ●Trade Associations: page 135.

If this fails:

* Get another firm to estimate (in writing if possible) for putting the defective work right. Note their comments carefully. These comments and the estimates are valuable evidence of the work done by the first firm.
* If the estimate seems reasonable get the second firm to go ahead and make good the defective work.
* You can then deduct their charges from the amount you owe the first firm (if you have not already paid their bill). In the case of repair work you almost always have to pay the disputed bill in order to get your goods back. So you will have to decide (bearing in mind the second firm's comments) whether it is worth taking legal action against the first firm to recover the money you paid to get their work put right. ●Suing: page 110.
* Alternatively you may be able to finish off the job yourself and deduct a suitable sum from the bill (e.g. half-finished decorating).

Uncollected Goods

Repairers have a right to hold on to your goods until their bill has been paid. However they do not have a right to *sell* the goods, unless a notice such as 'goods which are not collected after three months will be sold to defray costs' is printed on tickets or order forms or displayed in the shop.

The Disposal of Uncollected Goods Act 1952 gives repairers another way of acquiring the right to sell uncollected goods, but the procedure is so complicated that it is scarcely ever used. A repairer has to display a notice explaining the Act in his shop. He must write and inform you when the goods are ready for collection and write again a year later warning you he intends to sell the goods – only then can he sell them.

Servicing and Repairs

Buying a Servicing Contract

Many firms offer servicing contracts on domestic appliances or central heating systems. You pay a lump sum at regular intervals, for example each year, and (depending upon the exact terms of the contract) they may undertake to visit twice yearly to check the appliance and perhaps provide spare parts as well at no extra cost.

When you buy one of these servicing contracts both you and the firm are bound by its terms. If the contract states that in the case of electrical or mechanical failure an engineer will call within twenty-four hours to put matters right, then the firm is obliged to send an engineer. If they fail to, they have broken the contract and you are entitled to deduct from your final bill or next instalment any expenses incurred as a result, for example food ruined in a freezer or alternative heating costs incurred. See also ●Broken Appointments: page 58.

On the other hand if you enter into an agreement to pay for a service at regular intervals and you fall behind with your payments, *you* are in breach of contract and the firm is entitled to refuse to carry out their side of the bargain until you have paid.

Calling out an Engineer

If an appliance which isn't covered by a service contract

or a guarantee goes wrong and you call out an engineer to repair it, you will have to pay him a call-out fee, usually between £3 and £8. For this sum the engineer should give the appliance a thorough examination and diagnose any faults. You are not entitled to any repairs for this amount, though probably minor adjustments needing no spare parts will be covered.

The engineer should give you an estimate before replacing any parts, unless you called him out for a specific purpose such as 'Please come and fit a new control panel', in which case you should be prepared to pay for the work straight away.

If you agree to have parts replaced you are of course obliged to pay for them, and the labour. If you call out an engineer to repair your thirteen-months-old washing machine which broke down just after the guarantee had expired you may well feel disinclined to pay the resulting £20 bill. However you are obliged to pay it, but you should then take the matter up with the retailer from whom you bought the machine. ●Your Rights: page 25.

Broken Appointments

We all know how infuriating it is waiting at home all morning, or even all day, for a service engineer who promised to come but never turned up. An agreement that an engineer will call at a certain time is part of your contract with the servicing firm; if the engineer fails to turn up as agreed the firm has broken their contract and you are entitled to compensation. If more people realized this and actually claimed compensation, servicing organizations might be persuaded to operate more efficiently.

You are entitled to deduct from the final bill any expenses incurred as a result of the broken appointment, for example telephone calls, an extra trip to the launderette, some extra days of alternative heating costs *plus* any loss of earnings, if you had to take time off work. Make it clear when fixing the appointment that you will have to take time off work in order to be at home. Even if you haven't lost any wages it is reasonable to deduct a nominal sum (for example £2 for a whole day wasted, £1 for a morning or afternoon) from the bill for the inconvenience of having to wait in.

You should send a covering letter to the firm explaining exactly *why* you are not paying their bill in full, otherwise you may find they will refuse to deal with you again.

Contractors

Contractors include builders, plumbers, electricians, plasterers, decorators, etc.

If you are going to call in a contractor to do a job for you, get several estimates first. ●Estimates: page 53. Before you accept the estimate look out for exclusion clauses. ●Exemption Clauses: page 51. It is also a good idea to inquire whether the contractor has any insurance to cover any damage he, his employees or his bad workmanship may cause to your property. There is not much point in having a right to claim compensation from someone who can't afford to pay you.

A contractor is entitled to refuse to do anything that is unsafe or illegal, for example fit an electric socket in a bathroom. He should do the job in a good and workmanlike fashion and use suitable materials. ●What Standard of Work Can You Expect?: page 55.

Many firms ask for some money in advance to purchase materials; this is understandable. *Don't* pay the whole bill in advance. If the work is not finished or is inadequate you will have a good bargaining weapon or at least some spare cash to pay someone else to make good the defects. ●When Things go Wrong: page 56.

Cinemas, Theatres and Concerts

When you buy a ticket for a show, you are entitled to a seat in the position for which you have paid (e.g. front stalls). However, you normally have no rights if the 'star' does not appear – the management almost always reserve the right to make alterations to the programme. The conditions of booking are usually in the booking office, on the ticket or in the programme.

If you cannot find them, and the 'star' does not appear, it is worth asking for part of your money to be refunded. If no alternative entertainment is provided, then ask for all of it back.

You cannot demand any refund because you didn't enjoy the performance nor can you sue the critic whose rave review persuaded you to go.

Transport

When you pay to travel whether on a bus, a coach, a taxi, a train, a tube, a ship or a plane you make a contract with the company concerned. Even if you book through a travel agent your contract is with the transport company.

There are a great many laws, bye-laws, regulations and conditions which limit your rights – tickets are invariably issued subject to all these limitations. You can if you wish ask to see copies of the rules and regulations, for example at a railway or coach station booking office.

Trains, Buses and Coaches

A ticket does not entitle you to a seat. What's more, British Rail and most bus companies exempt themselves from liability if the train or bus is late or doesn't arrive. However they are legally obliged to accept responsibility for death or injury to passengers – if caused by the negligence of the transport company. Report any injury to an official as soon as possible.

Planes

If a plane is overbooked the airline you have booked with is in breach of contract. They should at least try to ensure that you get a seat on the next available plane (whatever the airline). They are liable to you for any expenses, such as hotel accommodation, which you incurred as a direct result of the overbooking. Airlines are not obliged to provide food or accommodation for passengers who are delayed, though many do.

There are complex international agreements laying down the maximum compensation payable in the event of death or injury. These maximum compensation figures are somewhat low, so it is wise to take out insurance.

Ships

Unlike other transport operators shipping companies can (and do) limit their liability for virtually every mishap – including death of or injury to their passengers. However passengers *can* sue individual employees who are negligent; the company (not the employee) will of course pay the damages.

Taxis

The rules about taxis vary from place to place. Local authorities control the licensing of taxis and the fares charged. Complaints in most districts should be made to the police, quoting the taxi's number.

All taxis have to carry adequate insurance covering injury to and death of their passengers.

If a London taxi stops when you hail it, the driver cannot refuse to take you to any place within a six-mile radius (or one hour's journey including waiting time) so long as your destination is within the metropolitan police area. The same applies to the front taxi in a cab rank, but does not apply to a taxi stopped in a traffic jam or at lights or to let a passenger out. From Heathrow Airport a taxi cannot refuse to take a fare to any destination within twenty miles and within the metropolitan police area.

If you book a taxi which fails to turn up, you can claim against the firm for any expenses you incurred as a direct result (for example the cancellation charge on a missed air flight). However you may have difficulty proving that the booking was made and accepted, particularly if it was made by telephone.

Hotels

A hotel proprietor is normally obliged (if he has room) to provide, at a reasonable price, food and accommodation to any traveller who arrives, even when no booking has been made. The proprietor can however ask for payment in advance and can turn away a traveller who is unable to pay or who is not in a 'fit state', for example someone who is drunk. This rule only applies to hotels which offer food, drink and accommodation to all comers, so it doesn't normally apply to pubs, boarding houses or private residential hotels.

Lost Possessions

If any of your possessions are lost or stolen when you are staying at a hotel, the management is obliged to compensate you in full, unless you yourself were to blame. The management can limit their liability to £50 per article and £100 in all, by displaying a notice (as laid down in the Hotel Proprietors Act 1956) to this effect in the hall or at the reception desk. A notice in the bedroom is no good. Furthermore, these limits *don't* apply if you deposit valuables with the management for safe keeping, nor if you *ask* the management to look after your valuables and they refuse, nor if the loss is caused by the default, neglect or deliberate act of the proprietor or his employees.

Cancellations

If you have to cancel a hotel booking the proprietor is entitled to claim from you the amount he has lost. Always confirm a telephone cancellation at once in writing. A hotel is not entitled to make money out of your cancellation, so if you can prove that the room was re-let and the hotel's losses were therefore minimal, you should only have to pay a nominal sum. Many hotels have a flat-rate cancellation fee of, say, 50 per cent of the price they would have charged. A cancellation fee agreement like this is only legally binding if it was a term of the original booking.

Double Booking

When you book by telephone it is a good idea to write a letter confirming your booking. If you arrive at a hotel to find that the room you had booked has been let to someone else and there are no similar rooms available, the hotel must give you a refund of any money you have already paid and compensate you for any extra expenses you incur in finding alternative accommodation, for example telephone calls and a taxi to another hotel. You must try to find accommodation of a similar standard – not book in immediately at the most expensive hotel in town.

Paying the Bill

A hotel proprietor has a right to keep your baggage until you have paid your bill, so if you are going to dispute the bill, try and remove your luggage *first*.

Travel Agents and Holidays

When you book a rail ticket through a travel agent, the agent's contract with you is really to make you a contract with British Rail. If the agent forgets to make the booking he agreed to make, you can claim against him. But if you are injured on the train journey you must claim against British Rail under your contract with them.

The same applies when you book through a travel agent for a package holiday run by tour operators. Normally the travel agent is merely responsible for making the booking. The tour operator is responsible for the 'package' – the flight, the hotel, the food and so on. Read the small print on the booking form carefully since it lays down the terms of your contract with the tour operators. ●Exemption

Clauses: page 51. Members of ABTA (Association of British Travel Agents ●page 140) have undertaken to restrict the use of exemption clauses in their contracts and not to cancel any holiday after the date when full payment is due, except for example in cases of war or political unrest.

If difficulties or complaints arise when you are away report them to the tour operators' representative in the hotel or holiday village, and if need be take them up with the tour operators on your return. ABTA may be able to help if the tour operators are members. They have a (potentially rather expensive) arbitration scheme, but you may prefer to sue the tour operators in the County Court. ●Suing: page 110.

If you feel the tour operators misled you about the holiday (for example by over-optimistic statements or pictures in the brochure) they may be breaking the criminal law. ●Trade Descriptions: page 94.

Sometimes travel agents themselves act as tour operators, for example by block-booking and re-selling hotel reservations.

Insurance

An insurance policy is a contract between you and the insurance company. Insurance contracts are contracts 'of the utmost good faith'. This means that you *must*, before taking out a policy, disclose all material facts to the insurance company, whether or not they actually ask for them on the proposal form. Any fact which might have made the insurance company charge a higher premium or perhaps even refuse to insure you is bound to be material. If you fail to disclose any material facts the insurance company is quite entitled to refuse to pay out on *all* claims made under the policy.

If an insurance agent fills in the proposal form for you, read it through carefully to make sure he has made no mistakes or deliberate omissions. Beware if he advises you to omit unpalatable facts, for example 'They won't want to know about that.' If it is relevant it's best to put it in, since if you don't disclose a material fact (even on the advice of an agent or because of his mistake or omission) your policy can be invalidated.

Insuring your Possessions and your Home

Read the policy carefully to see under exactly what circumstances you can claim. It is a mistake to imagine that 'comprehensive' or 'all risks' policies cover every eventuality.

You aren't entitled to make a profit out of insurance claims, only to be compensated for your loss, so there's no point in taking out two policies on the same goods, with different companies, as you can only be paid once.

Under most policies you can only claim the current value of an article – though under some 'new lamps for old' policies (which of course cost more) you can claim the cost of purchasing new replacements.

Check each time you renew your policy that you aren't under-insured. If your house is under-insured the insurance company is entitled to refuse to pay out on any claim. In practice they will probably only pay out a proportion of your loss. If for example your house is worth £12 000 and is insured for £6000, the insurance company will only pay out £1000 on a claim for £2000 worth of damage.

Motor Insurance

All drivers are required by law to be insured against liability for death or injury of their passengers and other road users. Many drivers also take out so-called 'comprehensive' cover which includes cover for damage to their own vehicle. Do check whether under your policy you have to pay the first, say, £25 of any claim.

If you claim under your policy you will lose your entitlement to your no-claims bonus even if you were in no way to blame for the accident. Some insurance companies do in fact credit the bonus in these circumstances, but you can't insist they do. It may be worth suing the other driver, ●Suing: page 110, rather than claiming under your policy – particularly if your loss was less than your no-claims bonus.

If you or a relative are injured or killed in an accident involving a 'hit and run' driver or a car user who is not covered by an effective insurance policy or if the insurers become insolvent, you may be entitled to compensation from the Motor Insurers Bureau, Aldermary House, Queen Street, London EC4, tel: 01 248 4477. If a 'hit and run' driver responsible for an accident cannot be traced you should apply to the Motor Insurers Bureau for compensation in writing as soon as possible and certainly within three years of the accident. They investigate the accident and decide whether to make a payment. You have a right of appeal if you are not satisfied with their decision or think that their offer is too low.

If the identity of an uninsured driver is known, the Bureau have a right to require an applicant to bring court proceedings against him and obtain judgment. The Bureau then pays the damages awarded if the uninsured driver cannot. More information can be obtained from your local Citizens' Advice Bureau. ●Who's Who: page 128.

Life Insurance

As well as your own life, you can insure the lives of other people – but only people in whom you have an 'insurable interest'. Marriage partners automatically have an insurable interest in each other's lives, otherwise (even between children and parents) you can only insure someone's life if their death will cause you financial loss. You could for example insure the life of a business partner, someone who owes you money or even the judge if you were involved in a lengthy court case.

There are many different kinds of life insurance policy. You are entitled to tax relief on premiums paid on policies to insure your own life or the life of your husband/wife. 'Endowment' policies pay a lump sum when you reach a certain age, for example sixty or sixty-five (or on your death if you die before that age).

'With profits' policies offer reasonable protection against inflation since the lump sum repayment includes a share of the profits made by the insurance company.

It is not advisable to take out a life insurance policy unless you intend to carry on paying the premiums. You can cash-in or 'surrender' a policy, but you are bound to lose by doing this. For the first few years a policy has no 'surrender value', i.e. you even lose the premiums you've paid. The company will work out a surrender value for you.

If you have difficulty paying the premiums, contact the company. They are often prepared to lend you the premium for that year. Alternatively the policy can be converted to a 'paid-up' policy (not normally a very good deal financially), i.e. a reduced lump sum is paid at the end of the policy period.

Electricity

Your local electricity board has a duty to supply you with electricity providing you live within fifty yards of the distributing main. You are responsible for the wiring, etc., on your property and the board can refuse to supply power if the wiring is not up to the minimum safety standard. You can be asked to pay in advance for any work the board carries out on your property. If you are a tenant your landlord is responsible for the wiring, etc., and payment in advance for work.

Deposits

The board has a right to ask you to pay a deposit before a new supply is connected.

Cutting Off

Your supply can *only* be cut off for non-payment of money owed for power already suppli d; *not* for non-payment of

HP or service charges. If you are cut off you must pay for re-connection, unless the board wrongly cut you off. In this case they are guilty of a criminal offence. Furthermore they should compensate you.

Meters

Meters are usually the property of the board – although landlords sometimes own meters in houses let out in rooms. If your landlord owns the meter you can find out from the board's showroom how much he is entitled to charge you. If money is stolen from a coin meter then the *owner* of the meter should bear the loss, not the person who uses the meter. It can be very difficult to convince your landlord or the board of this – but persevere.

Disputes

Each area has an Electricity (and Gas) Consumers Council (often called Consultative Council) who will help sort out disputes. Details from your local showroom.

Gas

The British Gas Corporation has a duty to supply you with gas if you live within twenty-five yards of a live gas main. You are responsible for any pipes which have to be laid on your land and you may be required to pay in advance for any work the Corporation carries out. If you are a tenant your landlord is responsible for the pipes and any necessary payment in advance.

Deposits

As for electricity.

Cutting Off

As with electricity the supply of gas can only be disconnected for non-payment of fuel bills. The Corporation must however give seven days' notice.

Meters

As for electricity.

Disputes

As for electricity.

Solid Fuel

Problems over suspected short weight, too much dust or poor quality fuel should be referred to your local Trading Standards department, ●page 129. If you have coal delivered, always count the sacks.

Any other problems which you are unable to resolve can be referred to the regional panel of the Approved Coal Merchants Scheme, the address of which can be obtained from the supplier or from the head office at 2 Turpin Lane, Greenwich, London SE10 9JA.

Post Office and Telephones

If possible, complaints about postal and telephone services and licences should be sorted out at local level. You can appeal to the Post Office Users Council, Waterloo Bridge House, Waterloo Road, London SE1, tel: 01 928 9458, but they are particularly concerned with issues which affect all subscribers. You may be wiser to address your complaint to the Chairman of the Post Office, 23 Howland Street, London W1, tel: 01 631 2345. The Post Office accept no responsibility for loss or damage to packets, parcels or letters (apart from registered ones), but the Postmaster General has wide discretionary powers to compensate consumers and it is always worth registering your complaint and asking for some compensation.

Hiring and Rental

Goods available for hire and rental cover a wide range: electric drills, prams, vans for do-it-yourself removals, TVs and telephone answering machines, to name but a few.

Whatever you hire you will almost certainly have to pay a deposit or a down-payment. The other terms depend upon the conditions of the hire agreement, which are normally printed on the form you have to sign. Read them through carefully before signing.

Watch out for the following points:

Looking after the Goods

Even if nothing is stated in the agreement (and this is rare) you, the hirer, must take care of the goods you have on hire. ●Looking after Other People's Possessions: page 50. Many agreements will make you liable for *any* loss or damage, for example a TV rental agreement may stipulate that if the set is stolen you must pay its current value to the rental firm.

Make sure you are properly insured. Household insurance policies often cover rented TVs. The hire firm often arranges insurance for short-term hirings, for example vans, sanding machines.

If the Goods don't Work: Repairs

Normally the hire firm is responsible for repairs and maintenance. Check the agreement to find out the terms.

You are entitled to deduct a proportionate amount from the hire charge if the goods are not working for a time during the hire period. If, for example, you hire a sanding machine for the weekend and it breaks down on Sunday morning, you are entitled to refuse to pay for that day or ask for a refund of money already paid.

Deposits and Down-Payments

You normally have to pay a returnable deposit in advance for goods hired on a short-term or day-to-day basis. The deposit is repaid once the goods have been returned undamaged.

For long-term agreements, for example TV rental, you have to make an advance down-payment of several months' rental charges. This is laid down in government regulations. Check the agreement to ensure you are not required to pay rental *over again* for these months.

Terminating the Agreement

This is only a problem with long-term hiring agreements. Check carefully that the length of the minimum hire period (which can be several years for a TV) is likely to suit your needs. If *you* want to terminate the hiring within that period the hire firm is entitled to charge you a reasonable amount for their losses. This might well be the full rental for the minimum period.

Check how much notice you have to give to end the hiring once the minimum period is over.

The Consumer Credit Act 1974, ●page 85, will, when the appropriate section comes into force, give you a right to terminate most hiring agreements after eighteen months.

Some agreements contain a clause which entitles the *hire firm* to terminate the agreement and remove the goods if you fall behind with your payments. Firms aren't usually keen to do this. If you are in financial difficulties approach the firm to see if they will agree to accept lower payments for a while.

5. Credit

Credit is used for many different purposes; to buy household goods, clothes and cars, to pay for holidays and to pay off existing debts. Mortgages are not dealt with in this book.

There are a great many kinds of credit, from bank loans and personal loans, through budget accounts, hire purchase and check trading transactions to 'tick' at the local shop. At the moment the different forms of credit are controlled by an enormous variety of legal rules. This means that your rights, for example with regard to cancellation and being told plainly the true rate of interest you are being charged, depend on what type of credit you use for your purchase.

There is a very important new law, the Consumer Credit Act 1974, whose various sections will be coming into operation gradually over the next few years. This will improve the legal protections for borrowers and set up a uniform system of legal rights covering most credit transactions.
● Consumer Credit Act: page 85.

Types of Credit

This is a brief summary of some of the main types of credit. If you are lucky enough to be able to choose the type of credit you use, compare the interest rates offered and the conditions which the lender imposes on you. For example, what are your rights if the goods you buy are faulty? Can the lender claim immediate repayment of the whole loan if you get into arrears with your payments?

Banks

Banks lend money to customers by means of overdrafts and bank loans.

An *overdraft* allows you to draw cheques up to a certain amount on your account when there is no money in the account to meet the cheques. You make your own arrangements for paying it off. Interest is charged from time to time on the outstanding amount.

A *bank loan* is a lump sum loan which you normally have to pay back in instalments, with interest, which is charged on the initial loan. The bank will usually require security for the loan, such as the deposit of a life insurance policy.

Budget Accounts

These are often operated by department stores. You agree to make fixed monthly payments and you are then allowed to buy goods up to a certain value. For example, monthly payments of £10 may entitle you to spend up to £80 in the store. You pay a small service charge on the amount you spend. This type of credit is known as 'revolving credit' – when you pay in you reduce your debt, which increases when you make your next purchase, and so on.

Check Trading

Examples are Provident, Bradford. The check trading company issues you with checks or vouchers which entitle you to purchase goods to the face value of the check. Checks are normally issued for small purchases; you pay a small deposit to the check trading company and repay the remainder in instalments over twenty weeks to the agent who calls weekly. Only certain shops will accept these checks. The check trading company pays the shop for the goods but deducts a discount, so often shops that take checks put up their prices to cover the discount. Interest rates are fairly high.

Check traders also issue vouchers for larger purchases.

Repayment is over a period of two or three years and is often made by banker's order.

Cheque Cards

These are issued by banks. The bank guarantee to honour any cheque up to £30 backed with the account holder's card. Many shops will now only accept cheques if accompanied by cheque cards. A cheque card also enables you to draw cash, up to £30, from any bank in this country and some banks abroad (Eurocheque Scheme). If you lose your cheque card and cheque book, report the loss at once to your bank. They can hold you liable for any money drawn on your account, if you don't inform them promptly.

Credit Cards

A credit card (e.g. Access, Barclaycard, Diners Club) allows you to buy goods and services on credit. The issuing company pays the trader, deducting a discount, and you pay the issuing company by instalments. In this way they resemble check trading. Interest can be quite high. If you lose your card you are responsible for any money drawn on it until you notify the issuing company. Most companies protect the consumer by limiting his liability to £25 providing they are notified at once.

Credit Unions

These are relatively new in this country, though popular abroad. You buy shares in the union and can then borrow depending upon the amount of shares you hold and your credit worthiness. Rates of interest are usually reasonable. Details from Credit Union League of Great Britain, 70 Pembroke Road, London W8; National Federation of Credit Unions, 10 Amity Grove, London SW20.

Credit Sale

●Page 78.

Hire Purchase and Conditional Sale

●Page 77. Conditional sale is similar to hire purchase. Compared with hire purchase it is very rarely used.

Moneylenders

These operate under annual licences, which are required by the Moneylenders Act 1927. They charge extremely high interest rates since they tend to cater for 'high risk' borrowers. They sometimes charge interest rates of more than 100 per cent. However, a court will not enforce a moneylender's claim for interest repayments of more than 48 per cent (true rate) unless the moneylender can prove the rate was not excessive in the circumstances.

Pawnbrokers

These lend money for short periods. You have to 'pledge' or deposit goods such as jewellery with the pawnbroker as security for the loan. Interest rates are limited under the Pawnbrokers Acts 1872 and 1960 to 25 per cent. If you don't repay the loan in time to redeem your pledge, the pawnbroker has the right to sell the goods. If more than £2 has been lent on the goods he must sell them at a public auction. You can reclaim any profit he makes on the sale.

Personal Loans

These are often granted by finance houses, or banks. A personal loan can be used for any purpose, even though it might have been granted for a specific purpose. Traders often arrange personal loans for their customers, to finance large purchases such as cars and central heating systems. You repay the lump sum over a period such as two years, with interest.

Beware of personal loans: the interest rates are normally high, you are obliged to continue your repayments even if the goods are unsatisfactory and many loan agreements require you to repay the whole loan if you fall behind with even one payment. You have *no* right to terminate or cancel a personal loan agreement. Personal loan agreements mean that you, the customer, do not get the protection of the Hire Purchase Act. See also ●How to Recognize HP and Credit Sale Agreements: page 80.

True Interest Rate

Finance companies and traders are not under any legal obligation to quote interest rates. If an interest rate is mentioned it may well be the flat rate, which is misleading since the true interest rate is in fact higher. The flat rate is worked out by comparing the credit charges (sometimes called service charges) with the total sum borrowed, on the assumption that none of the loan is repaid until the end of the loan period. Whereas in fact if you are repaying by instalments your debt to the finance company is gradually decreasing. The true rate of interest is calculated by comparing the credit charges periodically with the amount you still owe the finance company.

You can work out the approximate true rate by multiplying the flat rate by 1·8. For example, if you borrow £100, repayable in twelve monthly instalments of £10 each, by the end of the year you will have repaid £120. The flat rate of interest would be quoted as 20 per cent. The true rate of interest is in fact approximately 1·8 × 20 per cent=36 per cent.

Credit Reference Agencies

When you apply for credit you are normally asked to fill in a proposal form giving details of your job, your address, the kind of accommodation you live in and whether you own or rent it. The finance company normally sends the details on this form to a credit reference agency for your credit worthiness to be checked. Guarantors will also have to fill in a proposal form.

There are a number of credit reference agencies which collect information about bad payers from debt departments of finance houses and commercial debt collection agencies. Some agencies have details of good payers too. A lot of information comes from the Registry of County Court Judgments, 140 Gower Street, London WC1E 6HT. If you are successfully sued in the County Court for a debt of more than £10 and you don't reduce the amount of the debt to less than £10 within twenty-eight days of the entry of judgment, your name will go on the register and stay there for ten years. When you have paid off your debt you can apply in writing with a 10p fee to have your name removed.

If You are Refused Credit

No one has a right to be granted credit. At the moment a company is not obliged to reveal why your application for credit has been refused, nor do they have to say whether they have used a credit reference agency. Even if you do find out that they have, you cannot make the agency show you their information, although most will for a fee. If you find incorrect information you can apply to have it corrected, but the agency doesn't have to do so.

If you are refused credit any deposit already paid must be refunded, unless you made false statements in your application.

Your rights will be considerably improved when the Consumer Credit Act 1974 is fully operational. ●Page 85.

Hire Purchase and Credit Sale

How Hire Purchase Works

Most shops and garages don't have sufficient funds to finance their customers' HP agreements so they have an arrangement with a finance company. You choose the goods you want, fill in the HP forms and pay a deposit to the shop. The shop then sells the goods to the finance company and they in turn 'hire' the goods to you under the HP agreement. The shop keeps the deposit and is paid the rest of the price by the finance company. You have the use of the goods straight away (although the finance company actually own them). The HP price is paid to the finance company in instalments.

Every HP agreement gives you, the customer, an option (which of course most people exercise) to buy the goods from the finance company at the end of the 'hire' period, by making a nominal payment of, for example, £1. Only when that final payment is made do the goods become your property.

Until then you have no right to sell the goods without the consent of the finance company. They will normally only agree if you pay off all your instalments at once.

If you are thinking of buying a secondhand car, van or motor bike, and you suspect that it may in fact be the subject of an HP agreement there is a way you can check. ●Page 41.

How Credit Sale Works

Credit sale transactions are different from HP. In a credit sale transaction the goods become yours at once. The shop sells them to the finance company who sell them to you outright and you then pay off the finance company by five or more instalments. Since the goods become yours at once, you can sell them if you want, although most credit sale agreements require you to pay off all remaining instalments immediately if you do sell.

Advertisements

Advertisements for goods available on HP or credit sale must, if a sum of money is mentioned, give a complete picture of the financial terms. The Advertisements (Hire Purchase) Act 1967 does not make it compulsory for firms to quote interest rates, but if they do they must quote true interest rates calculated according to a special formula in the Act. As a result most advertisements never quote interest rates.

Deposits and Interest Rates

One of the means which the government uses to control the economy is control on the granting of credit. So government regulations are sometimes made fixing minimum deposits and maximum repayment periods. There is no legal maximum for interest rates. Remember the difference between the flat rate of interest and the true interest rate.
● True Interest Rate: page 76.

The Hire Purchase Act

The Hire Purchase Act 1965 provides important legal safeguards, explained below, for people buying goods on HP and credit sale agreements. The Act applies to HP agreements where the total credit price (deposit plus all the instalments) is not more than £2000, and most of its provisions also apply to credit sale agreements where the total credit price is between £30 and £2000, and is paid in five or more instalments.

Making the Agreement

HP and credit sale agreements are pretty complicated documents. It's often a good idea to ask several firms for specimen copies of their agreements to take away and compare the terms they offer.

Before signing an HP or credit sale agreement (within the financial limits of the Act), you must be told, in writing, the *cash* price of the goods you are buying – a price ticket on goods you inspect or a price marked in a catalogue is enough. Also the agreement itself must give details of the total credit price, the cash price and the instalments, so you can tell how much extra you are paying for credit. If this information is not provided the finance company can't enforce the agreement against you in a court, to make you pay up.

How to Recognize HP and Credit Sale Agreements

(1) Look for the red-printed box in which you have to sign. In an HP agreement this will contain the words 'This document contains the terms of a hire-purchase agreement. Sign it only if you wish to be legally bound by them.' Then there is a space for your signature. After that are printed the words 'The goods will not become your property until you have made all the payments. You must not sell them before then.'

The red-printed signature box in a credit sale agreement reads 'This document contains the terms of a credit sale agreement. Sign it only if you want to be legally bound by them.'

An agreement which does not have a red-printed signature box containing these words is *not* a hire purchase or credit sale agreement. It may, for example, be a personal loan agreement, ●page 75, or a simple hire agreement – under which the goods will never become yours, however much you pay. ●Hiring: page 69.

(2) HP and credit sale agreements which are signed off trade premises will have another red-printed box on them entitled 'Notice to customer: right of cancellation' and which briefly sets out your right to change your mind about the agreement. Other credit agreements or simple hiring agreements will not have this box.

(3) In an HP agreement the finance company is usually referred to as the 'owner' and you are referred to as the 'hirer'. In a credit sale agreement the finance company is usually called the 'seller' and you are called the 'buyer'.

The terminology will probably be different – for example 'lender' and 'borrower' – in other credit agreements. Look out for hire agreements as the terms 'owner' and 'hirer' may well be used.

Changing your Mind – the Cooling Off Period

If you sign an HP or credit sale agreement (within the

financial limits) at home – in fact anywhere apart from a shop, showroom or finance company office – you have a right to change your mind and cancel so long as you act promptly.

You can't cancel if you signed the agreement on trade premises, such as a shop. There is an exception to this rule. Some firms use the same agreement forms for customers who sign in the showroom as for customers who sign at home. If when you sign on trade premises the cancellation clause (look for the red box) has not been crossed out from the agreement form, then it is binding on the firm and you have the same right to change your mind as if you had signed at home. In other words the firm can agree to give you more rights than you are legally entitled to.

When you sign the agreement at your home one copy is left with you. Another copy of the completed and signed agreement has to be sent to you by post. If you want to cancel you must post a letter of cancellation within three days of receiving this second copy, so if you receive it on Monday, your cancellation must be posted by Thursday evening. Your letter should give your name, address and a reference number from the agreement and need simply say that you are cancelling your agreement. A name and address to which you can send your letter will be on the copies of the agreement.

When you cancel, any deposit or other payments you have made must be returned to you, as must any goods (or their value) which you gave in part exchange. If the new goods have been delivered you are entitled to hold on to them until your deposit and traded-in goods (or their value) have been returned. You are not responsible for returning the new goods – it is up to the finance company to collect them.

Faulty Goods

For goods on HP and credit sale, *whatever* the credit price, your rights are basically the same, and are against the finance company, not against the shop or garage where you chose the goods.

In credit sale purchases your rights against the finance company are the Sale of Goods Act rights which you have against a shop when you buy goods for cash. No exemption clause can take away these rights. ●Your Rights: page 25. So if the goods go wrong you must take your complaint up with the finance company as explained below for goods on HP.

In HP transactions your rights against the finance company which owns the goods are basically the same, but are under the Hire Purchase Act 1965. Since 18 May 1973 this has been amended to fall in line with the Sale of Goods Act, so since that date every HP agreement contains the same implied terms as ordinary contracts of sale do. No exemption clause can take away these rights. This means the finance company must provide goods which fit their description and are of merchantable quality (except for any faults which were pointed out to you or, if you examined the goods, faults which you should have noticed). Also if the purpose for which you want the goods is known, the goods must be fit for this intended purpose. ●What the Implied Terms mean in Practice: page 27. The law regards the retailer as the finance company's agent – which means any statements he makes about the goods before you sign the agreement are regarded as statements made by the finance company.

If the goods do not measure up to these implied terms you can claim against the finance company in the same way as you can claim against the shop when you make cash purchases. Notify them immediately of any faults.

In the case of new goods, if the finance company refuse to put matters right, you can deduct from your instalments the cost of any repairs and other expenses directly incurred as a result of the fault. Send a letter explaining your action.

The situation is not so simple with secondhand goods, such as secondhand cars. This is because secondhand items

can't be expected to be entirely without defects, so when a fault develops it is that much more difficult to show that the goods were not of merchantable quality when you bought them. You may have grounds for a claim if you were given misleading information about the goods.
● Buying secondhand: page 39.

Your Right to Terminate the Agreement

You have no right to terminate a credit sale agreement.

You have a right to terminate an HP agreement at any time as long as the total credit price is not more than £2000. But if you have paid less than half the total credit price you will normally have to pay compensation to the finance company.

You must give written notice to the finance company, surrender the goods and pay up all the instalments due when the goods are returned. In addition you will normally have to make up half the total credit price if you have not already paid this much. In fact this payment is only intended as compensation to the finance company for any loss they suffer because you haven't completed the agreement – they aren't entitled to make a profit out of your terminating the agreement.

If you fail to take reasonable care of the goods you are liable for any resulting damage caused to them.

If You are in Arrears

When you buy goods under a credit sale agreement they become yours at once. If you don't keep up your payments the finance company can sue you for the money you owe them, but they can't take the goods back.

Goods on HP remain the property of the finance company until you finish paying for them. If you don't keep up the payments the finance company has a right to take back the goods. This right is subject to two restrictions if the credit price of the goods is not more than £2000.

First, if an instalment is overdue the finance company must send you a warning letter giving you at least seven days to pay. If you pay within that period they can't take any further action.

Second, once you have paid one third of the credit price the finance company can't just come round to your house and remove the goods – they have to apply to the local County Court for an order. The judge, after inquiring into your financial circumstances, can make an order giving you extra time to pay the money you owe. As long as you pay the arrears within the time stated in the order, you can keep the goods. But if you don't pay within that time, the finance company can take them back.

In effect, an order like this extends your repayment period and so can be very helpful if you are in temporary financial difficulties. The trouble is you will probably have to pay the court costs. For this reason if you find you can't afford to keep up your payments it is much wiser to explain your difficulties to the finance company and ask them if they will extend your repayment period. Make an offer, in writing, of lower repayments over a longer period. If the finance company then decide to take you to court anyway and the judge *does* give you extra time to pay you are unlikely to have to pay the court costs as long as your offer of payment was similar to the order made by the judge.

Do remember that once you have paid one third of the credit price you are under no obligation to return the goods to the finance company, unless they have obtained a court order. They may well write to you if you are in arrears saying, 'We require you to return the goods.' If you do you will still have to pay the arrears and probably make up half the credit price as well. So if you want to keep the goods it is much more sensible not to return them but make an offer of repayment over a longer period.

Guarantors

Think carefully before agreeing to act as a guarantor for a friend's HP or credit sale agreement. If you are a guarantor and your friend defaults, you can be sued for all the money he owes. The finance company are under no obligation to try and make your friend pay before they sue you (though in practice they often do). You are of course entitled to recover the money from your friend. ●Being Sued: page 121.

Consumer Credit Act 1974

cover the money from your friend. ●Being Sued: page 121. gradually over the next few years. It is impossible for us to be precise about the timetable, so if you think your situation may be affected by one of the provisions of the Act, inquire at your local Consumer Advice Centre, Citizen's Advice Bureau or Trading Standards Department. ●Who's Who: page 128. The main purpose of the Act is to replace the current patchwork of laws with a uniform system of legal rules covering *credit* transactions of all kinds, e.g. loans, HP, credit sales, check trading, budget accounts, up to £5000. Transactions involving £30 or less will be exempt from some of the detailed rules. Similar protection will be given to people taking out *hiring* agreements which last more than three months, such as TV rentals, and under which the hirer won't have to pay more than £5000.

The local Trading Standards department will be responsible for enforcement of the new Act.

The Act will eventually replace many existing laws such as the Hire Purchase Act and the Moneylenders Act. Its main provisions will include:

(1) *Licences*: all credit granting and associated firms (for example brokers, debt collectors and credit reference agencies) as well as firms in the hiring business (for example TV rentals) will have to be licensed. The licensing system will be run by the Director General of Fair Trading. ●Who's Who: page 131.

(2) *'Truth in lending' rules*: false or misleading advertisements for credit or hiring facilities will be a criminal offence. Clear statements of the actual credit terms offered will be required – on the credit agreement itself as well – including the true rate of interest. All compulsory charges will be treated as part of the interest, except charges for services from a supplier whom the consumer is free to choose.

(3) *Extortionate credit charges*: the Act doesn't actually lay down any maximum interest rates, but gives the courts power to set aside agreements which are grossly unfair to the borrower.

(4) *Credit cards*: the mailing of unsolicited credit cards – except for renewals and replacements – will be a criminal offence. If cards are lost, the holder's liability will end altogether when the issuer has been told of the loss, and will never be more than £30.

(5) *Credit reference agencies*: a company that refuses you credit will be obliged to disclose, if you write and ask them, the name and address of any credit reference agencies who provided them with information about your credit worthiness. They must also inform you if no agency was used. They will not, however, have to give you a reason for refusing you credit.

If you write to the agency concerned, enclosing 25p, they will be obliged to give you all the information they have about you and to say where they got it from. You will be able to send a written request to the agency to correct any wrong information. If they refuse to do so you will be able to appeal to the Director General of Fair Trading.

(6) *Cooling off period, termination of agreement and repossession of goods*: the protection that HP customers now have will be extended to all the other forms of credit covered by the Act. The customer will have a right to terminate most hire agreements after eighteen months.

(7) *Faulty goods*: except for items having a cash price of less than £30 or more than £10 000 the lender will be

liable for defects when he has a business link with the seller. This will mean that nearly all credit purchasers (for example users of credit cards and trading checks) will be able to look to the lender to put defects right, as HP and credit sale customers can now.

6. It's a Crime

We saw earlier that there are some criminal laws which lay down rules that traders and manufacturers must follow. Your local authority employs officials (e.g. Weights and Measures Inspectors) to make sure the rules aren't broken. Traders who do break the rules risk prosecution in the criminal courts, and fine or imprisonment.

Most traders and manufacturers stick carefully to the rules, but sometimes the rules do get broken: usually by mistake or through carelessness, or, occasionally, deliberately.

If a trader breaks the rules – and you suffer – *he* may be prosecuted in the criminal courts, but how do *you* get compensation? ●Compensation for You: page 99.

Weights and Measures

The current rules are set out in the Weights and Measures Act 1963. The person to report any suspected offences to is the Weights and Measures Inspector, ●Who's Who: page 129, who is responsible for enforcement. Traders who break the rules can be prosecuted and fined.

The Weights and Measures Act:

* Defines a pound's weight, a pint's measure, a yard's length, etc., and gives local authority officers (Weights and Measures Inspectors) the job of checking the accuracy of weighing and measuring equipment used by local traders.

* Makes it a criminal offence for traders to give (even by accident) short weight, short measure or too few items (when goods are sold by number). Do watch scales in shops

and markets, make sure the petrol pump registers zero before the petrol starts going into your tank, and so on.

* Requires certain foods to be sold by *weight* (rather than by volume or number), for example tea, coffee, cocoa and drinking chocolate must be sold by weight. If prepacked they can only be sold in packets of 1, 2, 4, 8 or 12 oz, 1lb (or multiples of 1lb) or 1½lbs. If sold loose they can be purchased in any quantity you ask for. Many other foods also have to be sold by weight: meat, fish, poultry, cheese, most fruit and vegetables.

* Says some foods (easily countable) can be sold by *number* as well as weight, e.g. oranges, apples, bananas, tomatoes.

* Lays down rules about prepacked foods: most have to be marked with their weight or volume. So do some other items, for example soaps, detergents, toothpastes, perfumes, various toilet preparations, cleaning powders and polishes.

Unit Pricing

The Weights and Measures Act does not provide for unit pricing, i.e. doesn't require the buyer to be told the price per pound, per pint, etc. (no matter what quantities goods are *actually* sold in). It does require some goods to be sold in a limited number of prescribed weights, but many goods, such as breakfast cereals and biscuits, can be (and are) sold in packs of *any* weight. This means anyone who isn't first-rate at mental arithmetic really needs a pocket calculator in order to compare the price per pound and work out the best value for money. Standard pack sizes and/or unit pricing are badly needed.

Since resale price maintenance (the system whereby manufacturers could make traders sell their products at a certain price) was abolished in 1964, manufacturers can only *recommend* retail prices to traders. So obviously manufacturers can't price-mark products – this is the responsibility of the retailer. The Prices Act 1974 allows the government to make orders requiring unit pricing.

So far unit pricing orders have been made for some fresh foods, including fresh, chilled and frozen offal and mince, whether prepacked or not; all other prepacked fresh, chilled and frozen meat and some fresh, chilled and frozen, salted and smoked fish, not prepacked; prepacked and loose potatoes and many green vegetables sold loose. Other fresh foods, for example poultry and fruit, as well as types of fish and meat not already covered, are under consideration, as are standard pack sizes for biscuits and a reduction in the number of can sizes used for food.

Foods

The law controls the sale and production of foods far more strictly than of other goods. The main object of the Food and Drugs Act 1955 is to make sure that foodstuffs (and drugs) are pure, of good quality and hygienically prepared. We shall deal only with foods here.

The Act lays down standards not only for shops, cafés and restaurants, but stalls and vehicles (like ice-cream vans) from which food is sold; and premises where food is prepared, such as factories, bakeries and dairies and even slaughter houses and dairy farms.

Report any suspected offence to the local Public Health Inspector. ●Who's Who: page 130. Traders, cafés, etc., who break the rules can be prosecuted and fined.

The Food and Drugs Act (and many associated regulations):

* Make it illegal for traders/manufacturers to treat food in a way that makes it harmful to health. (This covers the use of dangerous additives during manufacture and preparation of food as well as bad storage.)
* Make it illegal to sell, display for sale, or even have in stock, food for human consumption which is not fit to eat. (This means it is an offence to have mouse-chewed biscuits on the shelves, or mouldy bacon in the cold cabinet.)
* Make it illegal to sell food 'which is not of the nature,

substance, or quality demanded by the purchaser'. (This covers such things as selling margarine to someone who asks for butter, selling watered down milk – both overlap with the Sale of Goods Act. ●Page 25. It also covers sale of food containing impurities, such as a stone in a pork pie, a cigarette end in a loaf of bread – this overlaps with the 'not fit to eat' rule.)

* Lay down detailed rules about hygiene in premises where food is sold, prepared or handled. There must be adequate washing facilities. No smoking is allowed near unwrapped foodstuffs.

* Control the composition of many foods, and the names given to foods. For example:

Pork sausages must contain at least 65 per cent meat, 80 per cent of which must be pork.

Butter has to contain at least 80 per cent milk fat, and no more than 16 per cent added water.

Spreads and *Pastes* are different: for example salmon spread must contain at least 70 per cent salmon, but salmon paste need only contain 70 per cent 'fish' though salmon must 'characterize' the paste.

Soft drinks: 'orange juice' must be 100 per cent real orange juice; 'orange squash' is for dilution, and must contain at least 25 per cent orange juice; 'orangeade' need not contain *any* orange at all.

We're not suggesting you could possibly tell for example whether the butter you buy contains more water than it should, but most manufacturers follow the rules because they know the Public Analyst does analyse test purchases made by the Public Health Inspector or the Trading Standards Officer.

* Make it illegal to put false or misleading labels on foods. (This includes shelf labels in the shop, as well as manu-facturers' labels.)

What's on the Label?

Quite a lot. Prepacked food labels are worth reading. The Labelling of Food Regulations 1970 and 1972 say that:

* All prepacked foods (with a few exceptions such as cakes, biscuits and foods in very small containers) must be labelled with a complete list of all ingredients, except water. The list must be in weight order, starting with the heaviest ingredient.
* Dry mixes (like cake mix): if anything apart from water has to be added, the label must say so *clearly*, for example 'Cake Mix. Add one egg and milk'.
* In addition to the brand name, a label must give a name or description to tell purchasers what the product really is, for example 'Goodegg. Custard powder'. For some products, like Oxo or Horlicks, whose brand names have become household words after thirty years' use or more, the brand name is sufficient.
* The advertisers and packers of foods and drinks for 'slimmers' are now limited by law to saying that their products are only effective as part of a calorie-controlled diet. Restrictions also apply to claims that a particular food or drink is a source of 'protein', 'energy', or 'vitamins', or is a 'tonic' or a 'restorative'. For example, high-protein bread must contain more protein than the average loaf.
* The label must give the name and address of the UK packer, labeller or importer (if the food is packed abroad).

Date Marking

A lot of shops stamp prepacked perishable foods with 'sell by' and 'open by' dates. These date marks are only meant as guidelines and many foods, if stored properly, can safely be eaten after the date mark has expired. At the moment it is not illegal to sell or have on display foods with an out-of-date marking. However if the food has gone off, or is mouldy or not fit to eat then the shop is committing a criminal offence under the Food and Drugs Act.

Some manufacturers put coded date stamps (supposedly for the use of shopkeepers) on their products. You will often find them on sausages, meat pies and pasties. There are many of these codes: for example

WO721   W=factory
O7=month of the year (July)
21=day of the month

H 23–3   H=factory
23=week of the year when manufactured
3=day of the week when delivered

O5J   O5=day of the month
J=month of the year (October)

A comprehensive system of 'open' (i.e. not coded) date marking for prepacked foods is under discussion at the moment.

Safety Standards

The Consumer Protection Acts 1961 and 1971 give the government powers to make rules about safety standards required for particular goods. Once a safety standard has been laid down it is a criminal offence for a trader (though not a private individual) to sell an article which doesn't comply with it. Complaints to the local authority (probably the Trading Standards Officer: ●page 129.

These Acts sound an admirable idea but there are several drawbacks:

* Not many types of goods are covered – the government hasn't used its powers very widely.
* No identifying mark is required on goods which *do* comply with the safety standards.
* Local authorities are not under a positive obligation to enforce this Act (unlike Weights and Measures, Food and Drugs) though most do.

There are safety standards for:
Oil heaters: they have to pass prescribed safety tests.

Guards for gas and electric fires, oil heaters and free-standing fireguards: they too have to pass prescribed safety tests.

Carrycot stands: they must be of certain dimensions and strength.

Nightdresses: children's nightdresses must be flame-proof; women's nightdresses must either be flame-proof or labelled 'Warning – Keep away from fire'. There are no regulations about pyjamas.

Toys: no celluloid may be used (except for ping pong balls); the lead and arsenic content of paints used on toys is controlled.

Electric blankets: they have to pass prescribed safety standards.

Electrical appliances: establishes the new wiring colours for all electrical appliances (brown/blue/striped green and yellow).

Cooking utensils: restricts the content of lead or any compound of lead in any tin or other metallic coating which is used on any cooking utensil.

Children's pencils and crayons: the lead content is controlled.

Spin Dryers: must comply with certain safety regulations, including limit on spin speed when lid is opened.

Trade Descriptions

Most statements made about merchandise are trade descriptions. The Trade Descriptions Acts aim to prevent traders and manufacturers misleading the public about their goods, their prices or the services they offer, by banning false or misleading trade descriptions. Offenders can be fined or imprisoned. You should report any suspected offences to the Trading Standards Officer. ●Who's Who: page 129.

Trade descriptions don't have to be in writing though many are, for example on labels, sales cards or instruction manuals. They can be given verbally by a sales assistant. Even a picture of goods in an advertisement (in print or on

TV), a brochure or on the packet can be a trade description.

Goods

The Trade Descriptions Act 1968 lists many characteristics of goods which *must* be accurately described. Misdescription of one of these characteristics is a criminal offence – in the words of the Act it is 'applying a false trade description to goods'. A manufacturer is liable if, for example, he puts misleading labels on goods or makes false claims in sales literature. A shop is liable if, for example, a shop assistant misdescribes goods to you. Shops can also be held liable for selling, or even having on display, goods to which a false or misleading trade description has already been applied, for example goods to which the manufacturer has attached a misleading label.

Characteristics which *must be accurately described* are:

* Size, quantity or gauge of goods: for example '6ft 6 ins' on an inflatable lilo, 'enough for 100 square yards' on a pack of weed killer, 'two gallons' on a watering can, '17' on a packet of envelopes.
* Method of manufacture, production or reconditioning: for example 'hand-made', 'heat-sealed', 'cut glass', 're-sprung'.
* Composition: 'woollen', '98 octane'. Description of goods by pictures on wrappers and packets often falls into this category and packet illustrations must *not* be over-optimistic about the characteristics of the packet contents, for example the amount of jam in the jam tarts or fruit in the fruit pies.
* How well goods will do their job, their strength, accuracy and behaviour: for example 'removes all stains', 'suitable for washing delicate fabrics', 'unbreakable', 'non-stick', 'noiseless', 'shock resistant'.
* Testing or approval by any particular organization, or conforming to an approved type: for example 'government

inspected', 'as recommended in *Which?*', 'conforms to British Standards'.

* Previous history of goods: for example 'army surplus', 'one owner since new', 'unused'. Many car dealers have been prosecuted under this section for selling secondhand cars with falsified mileometer readings.

* Manufacturer and place and date of manufacture: for example 'Royal Doulton', 'made in England', '100 years old', '1963 model'.

The Trade Descriptions Act 1972 also requires most imported goods labelled with UK names (e.g. place names, traders' names) or marks (e.g. trade marks) to have their country of origin conspicuously marked on them, for example 'Windsor Peaches. Produce of Israel'. There are some exceptions, like books, seeds and secondhand goods.

Definition and Marking Orders

It is somewhat pointless to outlaw false trade descriptions when many terms, e.g. 'mohair', 'camelhair', 'shower proof', 'crystal glass', which have no precise meaning can be used indiscriminately. The 1968 Act gives the government powers to make, for the benefit of consumers, orders defining the precise meaning of such words. Once a definition order has been made a trader who uses the words in a different sense commits a criminal offence. Unfortunately no orders have yet been made.

The government also has powers under the 1968 Act to require compulsory labelling of goods, e.g. 'leather' or 'synthetic' on shoes, washing instructions on clothes. So far no orders have been made, although the 1972 Act, ●see above, requires many foreign goods to have their country of origin marked on them.

Services

Descriptions of services, as well as goods, are covered by the 1968 Act. It is a criminal offence to give a false description of services if the person who gives the description knows it to be false or gives it recklessly (this means regardless of whether it is true or false, e.g. without bothering to check).

The description can be given orally or in writing or pictures (there are examples above). Services of all kinds are covered: cleaners, garages, employment agencies, travel agents, tour operators, public services such as gas and electricity, to name but a few.

Many kinds of false claims and descriptions are offences under the Act: false claims that dry cleaners provide a 'two hour cleaning service' (when in practice cleaning takes four hours), that a firm provides a 'country-wide delivery service' (but they won't deliver to Granny in Northumberland), that a car park is '150 yards from the beach' (in fact it's half a mile); false claims that a hotel has AA or RAC approval, that it has a bar or a swimming pool or that all bedrooms have balconies. Many tour operators have been prosecuted under this Act.

Descriptions of houses or flats by estate agents are not covered, since the estate agents are not describing services, and houses are not 'goods'. The estate agents probably would be liable if they falsely described services provided, say, in a block of flats, e.g. '24-hour porter service', where none existed.

Prices

The thought of getting a bargain is irresistible to a lot of us – for this reason it used to be a common selling practice for traders to offer goods for sale at apparently vast reductions. If a ticket read '£17 £11' there used to be no way of knowing whether the goods had ever been sold at the higher price at all, either in that particular shop or anywhere else.

The problem is not yet completely solved, but the Trade Descriptions Act has now laid down three rules outlawing certain misleading claims about prices charged for goods (but not services).

(1) A trader who claims he has reduced the price of goods must actually have been selling those goods at the higher price for at least twenty-eight continuous days in the last six months. Otherwise he commits a criminal offence. This rule applies to tickets like: '£17 £11', 'was £17 now £11', 'reduced to £11' (in this case the goods must have been sold for the requisite period at a higher price than £11).

Obviously if a trader makes a specific claim like 'last week's price £17, today's £11', the twenty-eight days rule doesn't apply, but his specific claim must be true.

Goods bought in especially for a sale (which of course won't have been sold in the shop before) should be marked as 'special sale purchase £11'.

Beware of phrases like 'elsewhere £17, our price £11' or 'Bond Street price £17, our price £11'. The Trade Descriptions Act imposes *no* legal obligation on a trader to be accurate or truthful about prices charged elsewhere. The same applies to phrases like 'worth £17, our price £11'.

(2) It is a criminal offence to mark goods at say '3p off recommended price' when they are not in fact that cheap. This applies whether the claimed reduction is printed on the packet, or is, for example, on a shelf label in the shop.

'Recommended price' means the price recommended by the manufacturers for that area. You can check the recommended prices of prepacked foods and household cleaning products in a monthly publication called *Shaws Price Guide* – your reference library or Consumer Advice Centre should have a copy.

However there is nothing to stop manufacturers inflating their recommended prices so as to make reductions sound more generous.

(3) It is a criminal offence to mark or advertise goods at a lower price than the price at which they are in fact for

sale, e.g. to mark tins of beans (on the shelf label or the tin) at 10p and charge 12p for them; or even to have tins of beans, some marked 10p, some 12p, under a shelf label saying 10p, and to charge 12p for *any* of the tins, or to have a poster in the shop window advertising cut-price washing powder when in fact the shop has sold out of reduced price packets and is selling packets at the normal price.

Compensation for you

A trader who breaks the criminal laws may be prosecuted, usually in the magistrates' court, and if he is convicted he may be fined (prison is most unlikely). Until fairly recently the only way for you to obtain compensation (if the trader was unwilling to give it) for any loss or damage *you* had suffered because of his illegal act was to sue him yourself in the civil courts. However, under the Powers of Criminal Courts Act 1973, criminal courts, such as magistrates' courts, can, in addition to fining or imprisoning a convicted trader, order him to pay compensation to the purchaser.

Anyone (not only the purchaser) injured by an article which doesn't comply with the safety standards laid down under the Consumer Protection Act, ●page 93, has a right to claim damages against the seller in the civil courts.

7. Complaining

General Rules

(1) First, sort out the basis of your complaint. If your complaint is against a shop which has sold you faulty goods (e.g. clothes which drop apart, appliances which don't work) you will probably be relying on the Sale of Goods Act 1893 and the Supply of Goods (Implied Terms) Act 1973: if your complaint is against a builder whom you have paid for work he has not done or hasn't done properly, you will probably be relying solely on your contract with him, not on any particular Act of Parliament. Your complaint may be about something which is quite legal, but which you feel is unjust – in this case a change in the law may be called for and you could make a report to the Office of Fair Trading, to your local Consumer Advice Centre, to the press, ●Who's Who: page 128, or to your MP. Reports and complaints made by members of the public recently resulted in legislation against pyramid selling.

(2) Decide what redress you can reasonably expect. For faulty goods: money back? repair? replacement? ●Page 30; for building work: partial refund? ●Page 56.

(3) Once you have done this don't waste time – *complain at once*. Delay can mean you lose some of your rights.

(4) Don't be put off if your opponent stonewalls you: if, for example, the shop who sold you the faulty goods tells you to contact the manufacturers. Explain their legal responsibilities to them.

(5) If negotiations fail you can sue, but you should regard this as a last resort. Although it is quite possible to issue a summons yourself, it is always best to try and reach

a reasonable settlement out of court, to avoid the time, trouble and uncertainty of court proceedings.

(6) Sounds obvious – but keep copies of all bills, receipts, order forms, letters, etc., and make a note of the names of the people you deal with (if they will divulge them!).

(7) Try not to lose your temper. It may make you feel better at the time, but can make your opponent determined to fight you to the bitter end rather than concede defeat early on.

(8) If in doubt, difficulty or in need of moral support – *get advice.* ●Who's Who: page 128.

Complaining about Services

●When Things go Wrong: page 56.

Complaining to the Shop about Faulty Goods

Let us suppose you buy an article which proves to be faulty. ●Your rights: page 25.

Go to the shop and tell them what has happened. Ask to speak to the manager if you get nowhere with the assistant. Don't be put off if they say they don't give refunds or tell you to contact the manufacturers. Explain that under the Sale of Goods Act 1893 they are obliged to supply you with goods that are of merchantable quality and fit for their purpose. Don't accept an offer to repair unless you are happy with it.

Remember that a complaint is most effective when made to the right person. Try to find out who has authority to refund money or deal with complaints. On small purchases this will nearly always be the branch or department manager. On larger ones it will depend on the size of the organization. Most major firms have customer relations or customer service departments for purchases that cause problems. They can often give a decision about a refund or a replacement which the branch may not have authority to do. However when you start going up the scale to complain it's normally best not to leapfrog to the top until it is clear the people lower down can't or won't help – otherwise you may well find yourself referred back to square one.

Writing to the Shop

If your visit is unsuccessful try a letter. In general, writing to the managing director of a major concern is not the panacea some people think it is as his secretary may simply hand the letter on to someone else, or even write back telling you who to complain to. Remember to include in your letter:

* details of the item, such as model number, colour;
* date of purchase and invoice/receipt number;
* date it broke or stopped working and briefly what happened.

For example

4 Leas Gardens
Walbridge
8th November 1974

The Manager
The Shoe Box
29 Broad Street
Walbridge.

Dear Sir,

re: *black leather zipped knee-boots*
style: Beatrice – price £17.00

I am writing to you about the pair of boots which I bought from your shop on October 8th 1974. The receipt number is B 5520793. You may recall that I telephoned your shop about the boots on November 6th and was advised to call. I visited your shop on 7th

November and spoke to you about the boots but we did not manage to get the matter sorted out.

I wore the boots each day for about three weeks after purchase. On the evening of November 5th as I was walking down the office steps, the heel came off the left boot. I fell, laddering my tights, grazing my hand and breaking the eggs in my shopping basket. I even had to go home in the flimsy pair of sandals that I wear indoors in the office.

I have not given the boots excessive wear, indeed I normally change into a pair of shoes or sandals indoors. The Sale of Goods Act 1893 says that goods sold should be of merchantable quality and fit for their purpose. I do not consider that boots which fall apart after three weeks' normal wear have either of these characteristics. I therefore cancel my purchase and would be glad if you would let me know by November 18th when I can return the boots to your shop and have the purchase price refunded, plus reimbursement of 80p for my laddered tights and spoiled shopping.

I am sure that a shop like yours will not hesitate to fulfil its legal obligations.

Yours faithfully,
Katey Brown

The Shop's Response

The shop may agree to your demands, or may make an offer such as a credit note, repair or replacement pair of boots. ●Page 30. If there are some weak points in your armour or the money involved is not a great deal, think carefully before turning down a reasonable offer at this stage. It could be a long hard fight to get a better one.

They may on the other hand deny liability – perhaps saying you have given the boots excessive wear. You could counter this argument by pointing out that the soles and heels are hardly worn.

Getting some Help

If the shop's response is not satisfactory, or they don't respond at all, it's probably worth trying to get some help from, for example, a Consumer Advice Centre or Citizens' Advice Bureau. ●Who's Who: page 128, for details and other sources of help. A second opinion can be very helpful – a person experienced in dealing with consumer complaints may be able to suggest a better approach or an argument you hadn't thought of; and it can often be much easier for someone not directly involved to mediate between you and the shop.

Trade Associations

There are literally thousands of trade associations, from well-known ones like ABTA (The Association of British Travel Agents) to less well-known ones like the British Horological Institute. ●List: page 135.

Many of them are prepared to help dissatisfied customers settle disputes with member firms. If the shop concerned won't discuss this approach, contact the appropriate association direct to see if the shop is a member and if the association can help.

Independent Testing

Some of the trade associations (e.g. SATRA for footwear) will test faulty goods when a member firm is in dispute with a customer. Technical appraisal can be most important in settling a complaint – particularly in instances where the shop is alleging excessive wear or misuse by the buyer. As well as trade associations there are numerous independent organizations which will, for a fee, undertake testing. Your local Consumer Advice Centre or Trading Standards department should have details. ●Who's Who: page 128.

If you can find a suitable organization and persuade the shop to agree (in writing):

(1) to be bound by the result of the test, and

(2) to give you a full refund (plus appropriate compensation) *and* pay the test fee if the test results are in your favour,

then this *can* be a useful means of settling a dispute. Remember you'll probably have to pay the test fee if the result goes against you.

It can be difficult to persuade the shop to agree to this course of action, and testing fees can be quite expensive, particularly with large items, like carpets, where people from the testing house may have to come to your house. Furthermore the result of a test can be rather ambiguous: 'the result of abrasion', but caused by what? and shouldn't the article stand up to a certain amount of abrasion? Remember that unless you request otherwise, the article may be ruined by the test. Make sure you know what is being tested – a suite, or a piece of fabric from the back of one of the armchairs.

In general, unless the shop belongs to a trade association which will do any necessary testing free or for a small fee, it may be preferable to sue and let the court decide whether or not an independent test is needed.

What Next?

The next stage is suing in the County Court. ●Page 110. Residents of Manchester and London have an alternative. ●Page 126.

When a Business goes Bust

Limited Companies

These normally have the word 'Limited' or 'Ltd' after their name. Check on their receipts, letterhead and in the telephone book. A limited company is an artificial legal 'person', quite distinct from its shareholders and employees. It can sue and be sued in its own right.

A limited company's existence is brought to an end by dissolution. Before this happens the company's affairs are 'wound up' by a liquidator, whose job it is to convert everything the company owns into cash and to pay as many of its debts and liabilities as possible. The winding up of a company can be voluntary or compulsory.

. Voluntary liquidation may be used where the company is still solvent, but the shareholders decide at a special meeting that the company should cease trading or move into another field. This is known as a members' voluntary liquidation. It can also be used where the company is insolvent and the creditors wish the company to be wound up. This is known as a creditors' voluntary liquidation.

Compulsory liquidation involves the filing of a petition at court (High Court or County Court depending on the size of the company) asking the court to make an order that the company be compulsorily wound up. The company itself can file the petition, so (among others) can a creditor, i.e. a person to whom the company has owed money for some time, and who has obtained a court order against the company requiring payment of the money.

If the court decide to make the order then the Official Receiver, Inveresk House, 346 Strand, London WC2, becomes the provisional liquidator until an official liquidator is appointed. The company usually ceases to trade, its employees are dismissed and control of its affairs is taken out of the hands of the directors.

The liquidator advertises for claims against the company, and then divides up its assets amongst the creditors. Secured creditors (such as debenture holders) and preferential creditors (such as the local authority in respect of rates, and employees in respect of a certain amount of wages) get paid before ordinary 'unsecured' creditors such as customers owed money, goods or services by the company. Shareholders of ordinary shares are bottom of the list.

Details of liquidations, receiverships, etc., are kept (together with other details about the company) at the Companies Registry. For more details see ●When a Business Vanishes: page 108. Your local Citizens' Advice Bureau, ●Who's Who: page 128, may already have been supplied with the details by their national headquarters. Otherwise they can obtain them for you free of charge from the Companies Registry.

If you are owed money, goods or services by a limited company which goes into liquidation all you can do is notify the liquidator of your claim, giving details and supporting evidence such as receipts, and wait and see whether you receive any payment. You cannot normally sue the shareholders and directors, because the liability of the company is limited to the amount of its own share capital provided by the shareholders.

In rare cases, such as fraudulent trading, there may be some right of action against the directors personally. It will seldom be worth pursuing such a claim, and in any case you should get legal advice first.

Once you have notified the liquidator of your claim you will probably receive regular progress reports and notices of meetings. It is not usually worth attending or voting at such meetings unless the company owes you a lot of money, goods or services.

Firms

If a firm's name does not include the word 'Limited' or 'Ltd' then it is probably a partnership or a one-man business. Each of the partners in a partnership is jointly liable for the whole of the partnership debts, not just his own share based on his share of the partnership. Someone running a one-man business is personally liable for his business debts.

A one-man business or a partnership can shut down at any time. But if either of these concerns is unable to pay business debts then bankruptcy proceedings can be brought. This is equivalent to liquidation of an insolvent company – the purpose of the operation being to convert the debtor's assets into cash to pay off his debts.

Usually a creditor sues the firm for money owed and a judgment summons is issued, followed by a bankruptcy notice. If the firm does not then pay the debt, an 'act of bankruptcy' has been committed and a petition in bankruptcy can be presented to the court (in London the High Court, elsewhere usually the County Court) in respect of the person running the one-man business or one or more of the partners of a partnership.

There is a court hearing to decide whether there are grounds for issuing a Receiving Order. If so, then the Official Receiver becomes the receiver of the debtor's property and the debtor has to provide details of his financial affairs. A meeting of the creditors will be held to decide whether to ask the court to declare the debtor bankrupt and to appoint a trustee in bankruptcy. If the court declares the debtor bankrupt then the trustee has to distribute the debtor's assets amongst his creditors.

As in the case of a limited company, if you are owed money, goods or services by a firm which becomes insolvent, you can only notify the receiver of your claim (with supporting evidence) and wait and see what (if any) payment you receive. Again it is not usually worth attending any meeting unless you want to, or the firm owes you a substantial amount.

When a Business Vanishes

What can you do to trace a business that has disappeared? For example the shop that was open last week when they gave you a credit note but is closed down when you return, or a building firm to whom you gave a down-payment whose telephone doesn't seem to be answered any more and when you visit its premises has 'gone away'.

Firstly, if you suspect deliberate dishonesty you should contact the police. Secondly, if you know the address of the business' premises you can try contacting the local authority rating department and asking for the name and address of the person or business that pays the rates on the premises. The vanished business may only be a branch or subsidiary of a larger concern. Be prepared to explain the reason for your request, since the local authority are under no obligation to divulge this information.

Thirdly, all *limited companies* have to register at the Companies Registry, Companies House, 55–71 City Road, London EC14 1BB, tel: 01 253 9393. The registration particulars will include, among other details, the address of the registered office of the company and the names and private addresses of the secretary and directors. These might be of help in tracing the business. Your local Citizens' Advice Bureau can obtain full details of the registration particulars from Companies House for you free of charge via their national headquarters. Otherwise you can call in person, telephone or write to Companies House. If you call you can inspect the company's file for 5p. If you ring you will be given the registered address but no other details. If you write you should enclose 54p (not in stamps) and ask to be sent the registration particulars of the company. It is *vital* that you give the company's name absolutely accurately, since the names of many companies are very similar. Companies House may be moving to Cardiff, but not until April 1976 at the earliest.

If the name of a *firm* does not consist of the full names of the partners, the firm should be registered at the Registry of Business Names, Pembroke House, 40–56 City Road, London ECIY 2N. So Fribat Builders, owned and run by Tom Friston and Ben Batley, should be registered. The registration particulars are similar (though no details of bankruptcies are given) and the inquiry procedure the same as for Companies House, except that the Registry of Business Names will not answer telephone inquiries and the charge for a postal search is 27p. Again your local Citizens' Advice Bureau can obtain the details for you free.

8. How to Sue on Your Own

If you have tried all the approaches suggested in the previous chapter without result, and you are convinced you have a reasonable case you can sue.

A word of warning – there is little point in suing a shop, firm or individual who will not be able to afford to pay up if you win. This is not normally a problem with a fair-sized business (unless it is on the point of financial collapse), but can be with one-man or small businesses. Don't assume that someone has plenty of money just because he runs a business.

Remember – the purpose of suing is to reach a settlement. Don't feel you *have* to fight to the bitter end; it's never too late to accept a reasonable offer.

Do you need a Solicitor?

●Solicitors: page 132.

It is perfectly possible to sue on your own without the help of a solicitor. There is a relatively new procedure in County Courts called 'arbitration', which is especially designed to help people who are conducting their own cases.

The details in this section will be brief. There are two very helpful publications which give many more details:

* *Small Claims in the County Court*. This is a free 74-page booklet issued by the Lord Chancellor's office and available from all County Court offices and most Consumer Advice Centres and Citizens' Advice Bureaux. ●Who's Who: page 128.

* *How to Sue in the County Court*. This book is published by the Consumers' Association and costs £1 for members and a little more from bookshops. ●Who's Who: page 133.

Costs

Before suing you should think carefully about the risk of having to pay your opponent's costs if you lose. The general rule is that the loser pays the winner's costs.

In general you only need worry about costs if you are claiming more than £75. If your claim is only just above £75 it is probably worth reducing it to £75 to limit the risk of having heavy costs awarded against you if you lose. Also your opponent cannot then veto your request for arbitration. ●Arbitration: page 114.

Claims under £5

No legal costs can be awarded. If you sue a shop for less than £5 and lose, you will not have to pay their legal costs, only their expenses such as witnesses' allowances.

Claims between £5 and £75

If you lose you can in general only be asked to pay a nominal sum towards your opponent's legal fees, plus expenses such as witnesses' allowances. Only in exceptional cases (for example if the court feels that your conduct has been unreasonable) can you be asked to contribute more towards your opponent's legal expenses.

Claims over £75

If you lose you can be made to pay a sizable proportion of your opponent's legal costs. The costs of a fully defended legal action can mount up rapidly, for example where £150 is claimed they could be at least another £150. The more complicated the case, the larger the amount of money at stake and the greater the number of witnesses – the higher the costs will be. If you lose an action, ask for the costs to be assessed at the end of the trial. Otherwise (and this usually happens in complicated cases) the bill of costs will have to be 'taxed'; this means your opponent's solicitor prepares a detailed bill of costs and you both return to court at a later date for the registrar to decide how much is to be allowed. Costs awarded on taxation are likely to be higher.

These are the financial limits from 1 October 1974. As they are reviewed from time to time you should check at the court office.

Warning Letter

Write a final letter to the shop reminding them of your previous letters, visits, etc., and summing up what you understand to have been their reaction to your requests for satisfaction. Conclude with a final paragraph like this: 'If, within fourteen days of today's date, I do not receive from you the sum of £17.80 I shall have no alternative but to start legal proceedings against you without further notice.'

Which Court?

Civil claims, such as consumer claims, are dealt with by County Courts. ●Civil Courts: page 19. When issuing a summons you can't automatically use the court most convenient for you. You must issue the summons:

either in the court for the district where your opponent, called 'the defendant', lives or carries on business. Limited (Ltd) companies 'carry on business' from their registered address. You can find this out from Companies House ●page 109.

or in the court for the district where the contract was made, e.g. where you bought the boots.

Particulars of Claim

When you issue a summons you have to provide the court with written details of your claim. These needn't be exhaustive, but should be written or typed clearly in numbered paragraphs, the last paragraph stating what you are claiming. Remember that when you claim damages you have a duty to mitigate your loss – in other words, keep your loss to a reasonable level. This means you can't claim taxi fares if you could equally well have gone on the bus. You will need one copy for the court, one for the defendant and one for yourself.

Here is an example – properly headed up:

IN THE   Walbridge County Court   Plaint No.....

BETWEEN   Katey Brown   Plaintiff

and

The Shoe Box (firm)   Defendant

(1) On 8 October 1974 I bought a pair of black leather zipped knee-boots, style Beatrice, for £17 from The Shoe Box, 29 Broad Street, Walbridge. The receipt number was B5520793.

(2) I wore the boots to work each day until, on the evening of 5 November 1974, as I was walking down the office steps the heel came off the left boot and I fell, laddering my tights, grazing my hand and breaking the eggs in my shopping basket.

(3) I contacted The Shoe Box the next day, but despite various visits, letters and telephone calls, the manager of The Shoe Box has refused to replace the boots or refund the purchase price.

(4) I therefore claim

    (a) a refund of the purchase price   £17·00

    (b) expenses incurred:

        stationery and postage   ·20

        telephone calls   ·15

        2 return visits to shop   ·35

        replacing laddered tights   ·40

        replacing spoiled shopping ·40

    (c) costs

(5) If the claim is disputed I should like the proceedings referred to arbitration.

| To the registrar of the court and to the defendant | Dated 1974
Signed ....
(Katey Brown) of 4 Leas Gardens, Walbridge, the plaintiff who will accept service of all proceedings at that address. |

Arbitration

Point (5) of the particulars of claim mentions arbitration. This scheme has been operating in County Courts since October 1973 and is designed to help people conduct their own cases without the services of a lawyer. It is a good idea to ask for arbitration if you are suing on your own.

The registrar of the court (a qualified solicitor) is usually the arbitrator. The hearing will be in private, not in the public court room, and will be much less formal than a court hearing. For example written statements from people not actually present may be allowed (normally witnesses have to give evidence on oath, so written statements, letters, etc., are not allowed in evidence).

Either plaintiff or defendant can ask for arbitration. When you are the plaintiff (i.e. suing), do this on your particulars of claim. If the claim is for less than £100 the registrar can (and probably will if you request it) refer your case to arbitration even if your opponent objects. For claims of more than £100 both parties have to agree. The arbitrator's decision has all the force of an ordinary County Court judgment. Appeal is only possible on a point of law.

Issuing the Summons

When you have prepared three copies of your particulars of claim, take two along to the County Court office. You will be asked whether you want an 'ordinary' or 'default' summons, ●Which Summons? : see below, and will be given a 'request' form to fill in.

You will have to pay a court fee in cash to take out a summons. The fee depends on how much you are claiming. From 1 October 1974 the fees are:

Amount Claimed (£)		Fees (£)
More than	Not more than	
—	10	1
10	20	2·50
20	50	4
50	100	5
100	250	6
250	500	7
500	—	8

They are of course increased from time to time, so check at the court office.

You can serve the summons on the defendant yourself, but it is probably more sensible to pay an extra 75p to the court for them to serve it for you.

When you hand in the completed 'request' form, two copies of your particulars of claim and the fee, the clerk will give you a Plaint Note. This has the number of your case, called the 'Plaint number' on it. Always take the Plaint Note when visiting the court and quote the Plaint number in correspondence.

Which Summons?

There are two kinds of summons:

Default summons, ●example, page 116, is issued if you are claiming a fixed sum of money such as the repayment of a debt or the return of the purchase price of defective goods.

Default Summons

<table>
<tr><td>22.—Default Summons.
Order 6, Rule 3 (2) (b).</td><td>Address all communications for the Court to:-
"The Registrar, County Court,

2 Market Square, Walbridge

WALBRIDGE **County Court**</td><td>PLAINT No.　75 11073

Which must be mentioned in any letter
to the Court about this case.</td></tr>
</table>

EASYLOANS LTD.
161a High Street
Walbridge

Plaintiff

(SEAL)

A.N. OTHER
123 Broad Street
Walbridge

Defendant

TO THE DEFENDANT

THE PLAINTIFF CLAIMS

		£	P
DEBT (particulars are attached)		22	50
COSTS { Court Fee		4	00
Solicitor's Charge			
	TOTAL	26	50

Judgment may be obtained against you and enforced without further notice unless within 14 days of the service of this summons, inclusive of the day of service, you:

Pay the total amount of the claim and costs into Court

or

Send to the Court an Admission, Defence or Counterclaim for which the attached form should be used.

Issued　3rd March 1975

John Smith
Registrar.

IMPORTANT—FOR INSTRUCTIONS TURN OVER

To the Defendant.

RM 1/72

Ordinary Summons

18(2).- *Ordinary Summons* Address all communications for the Court to:-
(Pre-Trial Review)   "The Registrar, County Court.   "
Order 6, Rule 3 (2) (b)   2 Market Square, Walbridge

WALBRIDGE   **County Court**

PLAINT No.   75 51073

Which must be mentioned in any letter
to the Court about this case.

A.N. OTHER   Plaintiff
123 Broad Street
Walbridge

SEAL.

PHOTOGRAPHIC SUPPLIES
49 St. John Street
Walbridge

Defendant

TO THE DEFENDANT

THE PLAINTIFF CLAIMS

		£	P
DEBT OR DAMAGES (Particulars are attached)		63	50
COSTS { Court Fee		5	00
Solicitor's Charge			
TOTAL		68	50

YOU ARE HEREBY SUMMONED TO APPEAR AT THE COURT OFFICE AT

The Court House, 2 Market Square, Walbridge

on   Tuesday 8th April 1975

at   10.30 o'clock when the Registrar will consider giving directions for securing the just, expeditious and
economical disposal of this action.

Issued   3rd March 1975

John Smith
Registrar.

To the Defendant.

IMPORTANT—FOR INSTRUCTIONS TURN OVER

RM 1/72

Ordinary summons, ●example, page 117, has to be issued if you are claiming a sum which is *not fixed*. The sums listed under point (4) (b) in the particulars of claim on page 113, are stated in money terms but they are *not* fixed since the defendant might argue they were unnecessary or excessive. So in this case an ordinary summons must be issued even though part of the claim − (4) (a), the return of the purchase price − *is* a claim for a fixed sum.

A claim for general damages as compensation for inconvenience, upset and loss of use is another example of a claim for a sum which is not fixed. You are asking for as much as the court is prepared to award. Such a claim could be included, in addition to (a), (b) and (c) under point (4) in the particulars of claim, ●page 113.

What happens Next?

This depends on what kind of summons you issue.

If you issue a default summons, it is possible for the case to be settled without a court hearing at all. The defendant has fourteen days in which to pay up or else return a form to the court admitting or denying your claim. The court will send you copies of any forms he returns to them.

If he does nothing within fourteen days, go and ask at the court for a form requesting 'entry of judgment'. The court will then issue an order telling the defendant to pay up.

If he admits your claim he may pay up at once or ask for time to pay and offer, say, £1 a week. ●Asking for Time to Pay: page 123. If you think his offer is too low you will both have to meet the registrar for him to decide how the debt is to be paid.

If he denies your claim (or puts in a counter claim), ●Denying the Claim: page 122, a date will be fixed for a hearing.

If you issue an ordinary summons, a date (shown on the

Plaint Note) will be fixed for a preliminary hearing, called a pre-trial review.

The defendant may offer to settle, perhaps by paying money into court. It is always best to settle before the trial if you can, even if you have to accept somewhat less than your full claim. Try to increase any offer by bargaining tactics. Any letters written should be headed 'without prejudice' – this simply means that if you don't manage to settle and the case does come to court, neither side can refer in court to the content of the letters.

If the defendant puts in a defence the court will send you a copy. He may ask for further details of points in your particulars of claim; don't commit yourself to details you're not sure about or which might damage your case.

The Pre-Trial Review

This is a meeting between you, the defendant and the registrar to discuss how the case is to be dealt with. Take all documents – bills, letters, etc.

If the defendant doesn't turn up you will probably get judgment in your favour there and then. If you don't turn up your case will probably be dismissed.

If the defendant does turn up the registrar will go through the case and may ask for some points to be explained. It may well be possible to reach a settlement with the defendant – if so, the registrar can enter judgment and the case goes no further.

If you don't settle, the registrar will discuss various practical points such as whether there will be an arbitration hearing or a formal trial, and what witnesses each of you want to call.

You can ask for 'discovery' of your opponent's documents: that is, to see and take copies of any of his documents, for example invoices, repair dockets, which you have never seen but which are relevant to your case. This can be very useful. He can also ask for 'discovery' of your documents. Your own personal notes prepared with your case in mind are 'privileged', that is, you don't have to disclose them.

If the registrar feels that an expert's opinion would help (for example the opinion of a local cobbler in the case of the boots, or a specialist mechanic in the case of a car or a washing machine) he may suggest that you and the defendant should try and agree an expert's written report before the trial. This is a good idea since it saves the expense of calling expert witnesses in person to the trial.

The Hearing

In many cases you and the defendant are the only witnesses. Any witnesses you want to call must attend in person to give evidence on oath – written statements are no good although the registrar may agree to accept them at an arbitration hearing. You can ensure that a witness attends by issuing a witness summons: ask for details at the court office.

Remember to take all your papers with you (and the faulty goods if they are portable). Prepare in advance a note of the main points of your case, including dates, times, places and prices. The judge will almost certainly allow you to refer to this freely. Also prepare a list of the questions (if any) you want answered by your own and the opposition witnesses. You can take a friend with you to the hearing if you want.

You will speak first. Explain to the judge you are a layman and ask for his guidance on court procedure. Go to the witness box when your case is called and, when you have taken the oath, explain your story from the beginning. When you have finished the defendant can cross-examine you. You can then call your witnesses (if you have any). The defendant and his witnesses then give evidence. You can cross-examine them. It's probably wiser to confine your questions to points you genuinely want answered and not attempt a devastating cross-examination.

The judge will normally give judgment at the end of the

hearing. It is a good idea to settle the matter of costs, ●page 111, at the same time. Bring to the hearing a list of any expenses you have incurred apart from the damages claimed on your particulars of claim, for example court fees, travelling expenses, cost of obtaining copies of documents. If you win an action involving more than £75, the Litigants in Person (Costs) Act 1975 provides that you can recover compensation for the time involved in preparing your case for trial, e.g. to offset earnings lost through time off work.

Enforcing the Judgment

If you win your case your opponent will probably pay up promptly. If he doesn't pay, the court can, for a fee, enforce the debt for you by a variety of methods. Ask for details at the court office – but remember none of these methods can get blood from a stone. There is little point in pursuing someone who has no money.

Being Sued

It is seldom a complete surprise to receive a summons. The most likely reasons are:

If you've deliberately not paid

For example if you have goods on HP which turn out to be faulty then it is normally in order (if the goods were new) to deduct repair charges and the cost of hiring a replacement from your instalments. ●Faulty Goods: page 81. This is only possible with HP and credit sales but *not* other credit schemes such as personal loan. The finance company must then sue you if they disagree.

If you can't afford to pay

If you are sued for money which you know you do owe, but you can't afford to pay all at once, you can ask for time to pay, ●page 123.

If you are responsible for someone else's debt

This can happen if you agree to act as a guarantor for a friend's HP agreement. ●Guarantors: page 85. If your friend fails to keep up the payments *you are liable* and you have *no defence* to the claim. You are of course entitled to be repaid by your friend and for this reason can ask the court to make your friend a 'third party' to the action. Details are available from the court office.

Receiving the Summons

You may receive the summons by post (recorded delivery) or a court official may bring it to your home. Whatever you do, *don't* ignore it – your opponent can obtain judgment against you if you do nothing.

There will be three documents in the envelope:

(1) The summons itself: it will either be a 'default' summons or an 'ordinary' summons. ●Which summons?: page 115.

(2) The particulars of claim, giving details of the plaintiff's case. ●Example, page 113.

(3) A form (no. 18A) of admission or defence. ●Examples, pages 124 and 125.

An ordinary summons

●Example, page 117. This will give a date for the pre-trial review. It is advisable though not essential to return the form 18A to the court within fourteen days of receiving the summons. You *must* attend the pre-trial review. ●Pre-Trial Review: page 119.

A default summons

●Example, page 116. This has no hearing date on it. You *must* return the form 18A to the court within fourteen days of receiving the summons.

Denying the Claim

You must have a valid reason for denying a claim. It's no good denying it because you don't want or can't afford to pay.

If you dispute the *entire* claim you should fill in the 'defence' side of form 18A, ●example, page 124. Remember to ask for arbitration. ●Arbitration: page 114. Continue on a separate sheet if necessary. Remember the fourteen-day time limit – particularly for a default summons.

If you dispute a default summons there will probably be a pre-trial review. In the case of an ordinary summons there is usually a pre-trial review anyway.

Admitting the Claim

If you admit the claim *in full* you should (if you can afford to) pay the amount claimed plus the costs shown on the summons into court within fourteen days. This should be the end of the matter, although in the case of an ordinary summons you may have to pay some extra costs.

If you only admit *part* of the claim then complete questions 1 and 2 of the 'admission' side of form 18A and (if you can afford to) pay the amount you admit plus appropriate costs for this sum into court within fourteen days.

Payment must be in cash, by money order or postal order. Cheques are no good.

Asking for Time to Pay

If you admit the claim but need time to pay, fill in questions 3 and 4 on the admission side of form 18A, ●example, page 125. If you already have to pay under any court orders give details of the court and the Plaint number. Give details of *all* other regular payments you have to make, such as insurance, HP, loan repayments.

Try and offer to pay off your debt within a reasonable time – but don't offer to pay sooner than you can really afford. Most people offer to pay in weekly or monthly

Form of Admission

18A.—Form of Admission, Defence and
    Counterclaim to accompany Forms 18, 19 and 22
Order 6, Rule 3(2) (c)

WALBRIDGE .... County Court

No. of Plaint........ 75 01439 ....

.... Easyloans Ltd. .... v .... A.N. Other ....

ADMISSION

If you do not admit this claim in full or in part or if you wish to make a claim against the plaintiff please complete the form overleaf.

If you have any difficulty in filling in this form, ask for help at your local Citizen's Advice Bureau or at any County Court office. Immediately after you have filled in this form, send it by post or take it to the Court office as stated on the summons.

1. Do you admit the plaintiff's claim in full?   YES/~~NO~~

2. Do you admit part of the plaintiff's claim?   YES/NO

    If so, how much do you admit?   ......£....................

    What are your reasons for disputing the balance?

Continue overleaf
if necessary

3. Do you want time to pay the amount admitted?   YES/~~NO~~

4. If you want time to pay, answer these questions:—
    PAY AND MEANS
    (a) What is your occupation? *fitter* ....
    (b) What is your basic pay before deductions? .... £ *32* .... per week/~~month~~
    (c) What overtime, bonuses, fees, allowances or commission do you receive? .... £ *4*
    (d) What deductions are normally made from your pay? .... £ *6.50* .... per week/~~month~~
    (e) What is your usual take-home pay? .... £ *29.50* .... per week/~~month~~
    (f) Do you receive a pension or any other income?   ~~YES~~/NO
       Please give details:—

    (g) What contributions, if any, are made by any member of your household? *£4 wife's part time earnings*

LIABILITIES

    (a) What persons, if any are financially dependent on you? Please give details including the ages of any dependent children
       wife and three children (11, 8 and 5 years)

    (b) What rent or mortgage instalments do you have to pay?   £ *9.50* ... per week/~~month~~
    (c) What rates, if any, do you have to pay?   £ *2.50* ... per week/~~month~~
    (d) Do you have to pay under any Court Orders? Please give details:—
       maintenance order to ex-wife £12.50 monthly. Tuiton County Court Plaint No. 66 71502
    (e) What other regular payments do you have to make? *Insurance £1 per week. H.P. on cooker £4 per month*
    (f) Have you any other liabilities which you would like the Court to take into account?
       Please give details:—
       Send £1.50 weekly to mother in Yorkshire

WHAT OFFER OF PAYMENT DO YOU MAKE?

Payment on the .... day of 19

OR   by instalments of   £ *2* .... per month

SIGN HERE .... *A.N. Other* .... DATE *14th* .... day of *March* 1975

Where should notices about this case be sent to you   { *123 Broad Street, Walbridge*

Form of Defence

18A.—Form of Admission, Defence and
    Counterclaim to accompany Forms 18, 19 and 22
Order 6, Rule 3(2) (c)

.... WALBRIDGE .... **County Court**

No. of Plaint.................. 75 11073

Easyloans Ltd   v   .... A.N. Other

DEFENCE

1.   Do you dispute the plaintiff's claim?   YES/~~NO~~

2.   If so, what are your reasons for disputing the plaintiff's claim?

(1) On November 6th 1974 I made an H.P. agreement with the Plaintiffs for a new SNAPPO SLR Camera, Model CR 1087B

(2) On Dec 18th 1974 the winding mechanism jammed. After examining it, the retailers (Photographic Supplies, 49 St John Street, Walbridge) said it would have to be returned to the manufacturers for about 6 weeks for repair. They agreed to lend me a similar used camera from their stock for £10 for use over the Christmas holiday. I notified the Plaintiffs in writing of all these facts.

(3) The repair bill was £12.50. I deducted £22.50 from my repayments

(4) This is the sum the Plaintiffs are claiming and which I do not think I should have to pay.

COUNTERCLAIM

1.   Do you wish to make a claim against the plaintiff?   ~~YES~~/NO

2.   If so, for how much?   £............................

3.   What is the nature of the claim?

                                                            YES/~~NO~~

NOTE: If your claim against the plaintiff is bigger than his claim against you, you may have to pay a fee before it can be
        dealt with. You can find out whether a fee is payable by inquiring at any County Court Office.

SIGN HERE: .... A.N. Other ....

DATE... 14th ....day of March .... 19 75.

Where should notices
about this case be   { 123 Bread Street,
sent to you   { Walbridge

If you have any difficulty in filling in this form, ask for help at your local Citizen's Advice Bureau or at any County Court Office.
Immediately after you have filled in this form, send it by post or take it to the Court Office as stated in the summons.

D P Ltd. 52-/358 5/73

instalments. There is nothing to stop you paying off more quickly if your circumstances improve. If your income is very low or you are getting social security you can write to the registrar and ask him to suspend the order for payment until your financial situation improves, or you can ask your local social security office if they will help you pay the debt.

Return the form 18A within fourteen days of receiving the summons, together with the first instalment of your re-payments if possible. If your opponent won't accept your offer you will both have to meet the registrar for him to decide how the debt is to be paid.

Small Claims Courts or Arbitration Schemes

There are only two in this country at present – one in Manchester and one in London.

They aim to provide a simple, quick and cheap way of settling disputes. Because these 'courts' are not a part of our official court system both parties must agree to submit to arbitration – in other words you can't force your opponent to attend. If he refuses you will have no option but to go to the County Court. The proceedings are conducted informally by an arbitrator, normally a solicitor. Legal representation is not allowed. The arbitrator can ask his own questions to find out all the facts and can arrange expert tests and opinions (e.g. a mechanic's report) if necessary, for a small fee. If you win your case and your opponent refuses to pay up, it is possible to apply to the County Court for enforcement of his debt.

If you win you will probably get back from your opponent the small court fee which you have to pay in advance, and he will probably be ordered to pay any expert's fee. If you lose you may be ordered to pay his small court fee and any expert's fee. These sums are small so the financial risk if you lose is not high (compare County Court claims for amounts over £75, ●page 111.

The Manchester Arbitration Scheme, 2 Ridgefield, Deansgate, Manchester 2, tel: 061 834 8896, will deal with claims up to £250. It is financed by a grant from the City Council and deals with claimants in the Greater Manchester area. The fee is £1.

The Westminster Small Claims Court, 153 Ebury Street, London SW1, tel: 01 730 3343, will deal with claims above £10 and below £250. It is run on a grant from the Nuffield Foundation and prefers to deal with cases in the Greater London Council area. The court fee is £5 for claims under £100 and £10 for claims between £100 and £250.

9. Getting Some Help

Don't hesitate to seek advice and if necessary help with your problem, but make sure the person you ask knows what they are talking about. Advice from somebody experienced in consumer matters may be more helpful than anything your neighbour suggests.

In this section you will find details of consumer organizations and other possible sources of advice, including a list of some well-known trade associations. Remember an impartial third party can often find a satisfactory solution to a problem that to you seemed insoluble.

Who's Who

Consumer Advice Centres

There are about seventy of these in the UK, usually in large towns. Often they are run by local authorities. Most keep copies of *Which?* and other Consumers' Association publications. Their staff are trained to give specialist advice and help on shopping problems and queries of all kinds. Most will give pre-shopping advice (e.g. will help you to choose the right type of carpet/toaster/TV for your needs and your budget) as well as advice on complaints. Most will take up complaints for you. Some are very strict about only dealing with residents of or shops within their district. Your Town Hall should be able to give details.

Citizens' Advice Bureaux

There are over 600 CABx in the UK. They will deal with inquiries on any topic, e.g. housing, social security, income

tax, employment, immigration and consumer problems.
Their national headquarters in London provides all
bureaux with up-to-date information about new legislation, etc. Individual bureaux are usually dependent upon
the local authority for finance – this largely accounts for the
variation in standard of service provided. A lot of bureaux
will give first-rate help and advice with consumer complaints, many will take up complaints for you and some
have solicitors you can consult free; others may not have
enough staff or resources to be so helpful. Find them under
Citizens' Advice Bureau in the phone book. Check their
opening times.

Trading Standards Officers

Trading Standards Officers are employed by local authorities to enforce the Trade Descriptions and Consumer
Protection Acts. Some also deal with Food and Drugs
legislation although this is usually the Public Health
Inspector's job. They make routine inspections of shops
and other retail premises as well as dealing with complaints from members of the public about possible offences
against the laws which they enforce.

Some Trading Standards departments also have Consumer Protection Officers or Consumer Advisory Officers
who are prepared to advise shoppers on civil law problems too, such as faulty goods. Some refer complaints of
this kind to other advisory services, such as the local
Citizens' Advice Bureaux and Consumer Advice Centres.

Contacting the Trading Standards Officer, ●see under
Public Health Inspectors.

Weights and Measures Inspectors

Weights and Measures Inspectors usually work from the
same office as Trading Standards Officers and in some cases
are one and the same person. Their job is to enforce the
Weights and Measures Act 1963. Their work includes making routine inspections to check weighing or measuring

equipment used in some way by the public (e.g. scales in shops, petrol pumps, measures in pubs) and investigating complaints by members of the public who feel they have been given short weight or measure. They also make random test purchases of prepacked goods which are sold by weight, volume or number.

Contacting the Weights and Measures Inspector, ●see under Public Health Inspectors.

Public Health Inspectors

Public Health Inspectors or Environmental Health Officers are employed by local authorities, usually to enforce the Food and Drugs Act and the many regulations governing the hygiene of premises where food is sold, served or prepared. (They also enforce legislation relating to health hazards in houses, such as inadequate sanitation, mice and damp.) They make routine inspections of premises such as shops, pubs and restaurants and places such as bakeries where food is prepared. In addition they make test purchases and deal with complaints from the public about, for example, mouldy or contaminated food, or mouse droppings or excessive dirt in food shops or restaurants.

Contact the Public Health Inspector, Weights and Measures Inspector and Trading Standards Officer through your Town Hall. The last two probably work in the Trading Standards department. The Public Health Inspector may now work under the Housing department or the Trading Standards department. Report any suspected offence to the appropriate officer as well as the trader concerned. The more information the officers have on trading practices within their area, the better they can protect the public. Make sure you keep possession of your evidence if you can; for example shops will usually replace, or give refunds for, mouldy food at once, but don't part with the food until the Public Health Inspector has seen it. Offending traders can be prosecuted in the local magistrates' court. Remember the local authority officers only deal with complaints about shops, pubs, etc., which are in their area, regardless of where you live.

Public Analyst

Every local authority must appoint a Public Analyst, although most don't employ one full-time but regularly use the services of a local consulting chemist or analyst. As well as testing food and drink for the local authority under the Food and Drugs legislation (for example: do any of the samples of butter collected by the Trading Standards officer from shops all over the district contain more than the legally permitted percentage of water or do they contain any margarine?) he also acts as the local authority's general scientific adviser. They will ask him to help with Trade Descriptions Act problems (are the 'all wool' blankets on sale in the local store in fact 30 per cent nylon?); to check lead and cadmium levels in cooking utensils or paint for children's toys; to keep a watch on possible contamination in water supplies and to monitor atmospheric pollution. For the last few years Public Analysts all over the country have done an annual national survey of pesticide levels in foods.

Analysts who are not employed full-time by the local authority deal with many queries from private individuals; for a fee they will test anything from the stubborn stain on your favourite dress to a meal prepared by a suspected poisoner!

Office of Fair Trading
Chancery House, Chancery Lane, London WC1.

This government office was set up under the Fair Trading Act 1973. The job of the Director General of Fair Trading and his staff is to investigate aspects of monopolies and mergers, and to safeguard the economic interests of consumers by recommending new legislation, publicizing consumers' existing rights and collecting information about unfair trading practices. The office *does not* take up individual consumer problems but may well be interested to hear about them – whether they have been solved satisfactorily or not, and whether they concern consumers' economic interests or other matters such as health and safety. You can make a report to the Office of Fair Trading via your local Citizens' Advice Bureau, Consumer Advice Centre, or Trading Standards department, if you wish.

The Director General of Fair Trading now has the extra job of administering the Consumer Credit Act. ●Page 85.

National Consumer Council
18 Victoria Park Square, Bethnal Green, London E2

This government-financed agency does not help with individual problems, nor does it do any research or testing. Its object is to represent consumers at a national level. It will make representation to both government and private industry on matters affecting consumers, such as legislation, local consumer advice services and improvement of the various voluntary codes of practice which exist in many industries, for example advertising.

Solicitors

It is not really financially worthwhile paying for a solicitor to deal with a consumer problem unless there is a sizable amount of money involved and the problem is a fairly complex one. Many people feel that a solicitor's letter will make their opponents give in immediately, irrespective of the merits of their case. This is not true and, particularly if your opponent is a company with its own solicitors, it can result in a long exchange of solicitors' letters. Opponents who give in on receipt of a solicitor's letter will probably do the same on receipt of a County Court summons and it is quite possible to issue a summons yourself. ●Suing: page 110.

If you are doubtful about your case it can be useful to ask a solicitor's advice first and then go it alone.

You may be eligible for Legal Aid (further details in

Legal Rights by Henry Hodge, another book in this series) but remember that if a solicitor handles your case any compensation you receive may be subject to deductions to meet some of your legal costs.

Law Centres

These centres are mainly in urban areas, particularly London. They range from Legal Advice Centres open one evening a week in a local church hall to Law Centres offering a twenty-four hour service and having several salaried full-time solicitors. Their services are usually free and intended for people who might not otherwise get legal help. They do not deal primarily with consumer problems, but may be a useful source of legal advice.

Consumers' Association

14 Buckingham Street, London WC2N 6S, tel: 01 839 1222.

This is the largest consumer organization in the country with over 600 000 members. Basic membership costs £3·75 per annum; for this you receive membership services and monthly copies of *Which?*, a magazine with test reports, value for money recommendations and articles about issues of interest to consumers. You can also subscribe to any of the *Which?* supplements, 'Motoring', 'Money', 'Holiday' and 'Handyman'.

They also publish a number of useful books (approximately £1 each) such as *Buying Secondhand, How to Sue in the County Court, Adoption, Coping with Disablement.* Publications can be ordered from booksellers or Consumers' Association, Caxton Hill, Hertford. *Which?* can be read in most reference libraries.

Consumer Council

This no longer exists. It was a government agency set up in 1963 and closed in 1971.

National Federation of Consumer Groups
61 Valentine Road, Birmingham B14 7AJ, tel: 021 444 6010.

There are local consumer groups all over this country. Membership of a local group costs about £1 a year. Groups usually concentrate on local issues which interest members such as surveys of local shops or restaurants or a campaign for a car-free pedestrian shopping precinct. The National Federation also organizes regular national campaigns on consumer matters. All members get monthly newsheets and most local groups produce regular bulletins. Many will help members with consumer complaints.

Housewives Trust
3 Sloane Terrace Mansions, London SW1X 9DG, tel: 01 730 2055.

This is an independent watchdog organization. Members receive the magazine *Insight* six times a year, and help and advice with their complaints.

National Consumer Protection Council
16 Woodward Avenue, London NW4, tel: 01 202 5787.

This organization will handle complaints involving goods or services. There is no membership fee, but you will be asked to make a contribution if you are given advice or help.

The Media

Nowadays consumers' rights and problems are being given an increasing amount of press, radio and TV coverage. A large number of national papers and magazines run fairly regular consumer features, as do many local papers. Radio and TV stations, both local and national, run programmes which provide information about consumers' rights, about purchasing and give details of listeners' consumer problems.

Most of these articles and programmes are a useful source of information, but few actually provide a practical means of solving individual consumer problems on a large scale. There are now very few readers' services that are actually able to take up a problem for you unless they intend to publish the story. However, if you have a consumer problem which you think it might help other people to know about, or which you think the media might be able to help resolve, don't hesitate to contact them – so long as you are happy for the issue to get publicity.

Trade Associations and Professional Bodies

Listed below are a few organizations who might be able to assist you with a complaint. There are thousands more, so if you cannot find one here that appears to deal with your problems, look at the Directory of British Trade Associations in your local reference library.

Building Services

National House Building Council
58 Portland Place, London W1N 4BU.
Tel: 01 387 7201
Has a register of private house builders and developers and gives a ten-year guarantee to houses built by its members. The Council will handle complaints about houses and builders covered by the scheme.

National Federation of Master Painters and Decorators
5 Haywra Street, Harrogate, Yorks HG1 5BL.
Tel: Harrogate 65292
2600 member firms. Will investigate complaints and arbitrate if necessary.

Electrical Contractors Association
55 Catherine Place, London SW1E 6ET.
Tel: 01 828 2932
Will handle complaints about member firms if made in writing within twelve months.

Heating & Ventilating Contractors Association
Coastal Chambers, 172 Buckingham Palace Road, London SW1.
Tel: 01 730 8248
Will take up complaints against members.

National Heating Consultancy
188 Albany Street, London NW1.
Tel: 01 388 0862
Will investigate complaints about defective heating installations, negotiate with installer and arbitrate if necessary. Their inspection charge is £3 per hour plus expenses.

Carpets and Flooring

Federation of British Carpet Manufacturers
Dorland House, 14–16 Regent Street, London SW1Y 4PR.
Tel: 01 930 8711
Will consider allegations of faulty manufacture or materials for British-made carpets. Arbitration can be arranged and all expenses are paid by the commercial party.

Retail Trading Standards Association
360–6 Oxford Street, London W1N 0BT.
Tel: 01 629 9314
Advice on complaints about carpets.

Contract Flooring Association
376 Gray's Inn Road, London WC1X 8DB.
Tel: 01 278 9608
Will deal with complaints, in writing, about members and non-members but make a charge of up to £30 for latter.

Cars and Motoring

Automobile Association
Fanum House, Basingstoke, Hants RG21 2EA.
Tel: Basingstoke 20123

Royal Automobile Club
83–5 Pall Mall, London SW1 5HW.
Tel: 01 930 4343
Both provide a technical advice service for members and will carry out inspections for a fee. Will deal with complaints against approved garages listed in their handbooks.

British Vehicle Rental and Leasing Association
47 Windsor Road, Slough, Bucks.
Tel: Slough 31028
Complaints about car hire firms.

Council for Vehicle Servicing and Repairs
94 Park Lane, London W1Y 3TA.
Tel: 01 491 7060
Will help in any dispute arising between motorist and garage regarding repairs or faults in a new or used car during manufacturer's or dealer's warranty period. Will give advice on where to seek help and will follow the progress of a complaint.

Institute of Automobile Assessors
c/o Institution of Mechanical Engineers
1 Birdcage Walk, London SW1.
Tel: 01 839 1211
Will provide an assessor to draw up a report for use at arbitration.

Motor Agents Association (new and secondhand cars)
201 Great Portland Street, London W1 6AB.
Tel: 01 680 9122
Investigation and arbitration service for complaints against member garages. Complaints must be made within three months of transaction.

Society of Motor Manufacturers and Traders
Forbes House, Halkin Street, London SW1.
Tel: 01 235 7000
Will deal with complaints about new vehicles.

Doorstep Sales

Direct Sales and Service Association
47 Windsor Road, Slough, Bucks.
Tel: Slough 31020
Will deal with complaints against members.

Dry Cleaning and Laundry

National Association of Launderette Owners
77 New Bond Street, London W1.
Tel: 01 493 3321
Will advise on complaints about members and try and help
with non-member firms.

Association of British Launderers and Dry Cleaners
319 Pinner Road, Harrow, Middlesex.
Tel: 01 863 7755
Will take up complaints made in writing against members.
Most big laundries and dry cleaners do belong.

Fuel

Domestic Coal Consumers Council
Thames House South, Millbank, London SW1P 4QEW.
Tel: 01 222 7000, Ext. 1220
Will deal with complaints about solid fuel supply. If complaint is about service try The Approved Coal Merchants
Scheme, Derbyshire House, St Chads Street, WC1, tel:
01 837 8630. They will put you in touch with your local
office. Members of the scheme are obliged to investigate all
complaints.

Electricity Consumers Council
(address in local showrooms)
A statutory body set up under the Electricity Acts – there
is a council attached to each board, who will handle
written or telephoned complaints. Try area board first.

Gas Consumers Council
(address in local showrooms)
Under the Gas Act there are twelve consultative councils attached to area gas boards. They will consider complaints about supply, and gas appliances bought from showrooms.

Furniture

National Association of Retail Furnishers
3 Berners Street, London W1.
Tel: 01 636 1778
Will deal with complaints including those involving floor coverings.

Mail Order

Mail Order Traders Association of Great Britain
507 Corn Exchange Buildings, Fenwick Street, Liverpool LR2 7RA.
Tel: 051 236 7581
Will deal with complaints against members, who include most of the well-known catalogue names.

Advertising Standards Authority

1 Bell Yard, London WC2A 2JX.
Tel: 01 242 4111
Will take up any complaints to do with advertisements. Especially useful when you send away for something from a newspaper or magazine and it doesn't arrive.

Shoes

National Shoe Retailers Council
Leather Trade House, 9 St Thomas Street, London SE1.
Tel: 01 407 5281
Advice available on problems associated with footwear purchase and with complaints in wear.

SATRA (Shoe and Allied Trades Research Association)
Rockingham Road, Kettering, Northants.
Tel: Kettering 3151
Will not receive complaints from the public. If you are sure
you have a good case, ask the shop to submit the shoes for
testing. Remember, the loser pays the cost of the test.

Television and Radio

Radio and Television Retailers Association
100 St Martin's Lane, London WC2 4BD.
Tel: 01 836 1463
RTRA Customer Advisory Panel will deal with complaints about goods and servicing of members. Represents
3500 retailers and distributors.

Travel

Airline Users Committee
Room 308, Aviation House, 129 Kingsway, London
WC2B 6NN.
Tel: 01 405 6922, Ext. 412
Will advise consumers with travel complaints, if no satis-
faction gained from complaint to airline concerned.

Association of British Travel Agents
50 Newman Street, London W1P 4AH.
Tel: 01 580 8281
Most large travel agents and tour operators are members
and the association will investigate complaints made by the
public.

Legal Rights

Henry Hodge

Legal Rights will tell you
* where to go for help and advice
* how to get legal aid
* how courts and tribunals work
* how to deal with problems over your family, your money
  or your home
* what rights you have as an employee and as a consumer
* what to do if you are in trouble with the police

Supplementary Benefit Rights

by Ruth Lister

Supplementary Benefit Rights will tell you
* how to claim your supplementary benefit
* how much benefit you should be getting
* how to get more than the basic rate
* what to do if your benefit is reduced, refused or stopped
* how to appeal if you're not satisfied

Born to Fail?

by Peter Wedge and Hilary Prosser

The National Children's Bureau reports on striking differences in the lives of British children

Of all the children born in Britain in the week of 3–9 March 1958

* ★ 1 in 4 have grown up in a family with 5 or more children or with only one parent
* ★ 1 in 4 have been living in bad housing
* ★ 1 in 7 have been in low income families

Any one of these experiences may be hard enough for a child to overcome

But 1 in 16 children – on average 2 in every British classroom – have to face all three situations

Born to Fail? shows the massive accumulation of additional hardships that confront this group of children in almost every aspect of their daily lives.

What do we expect to become of them?
What should we do to help them?

An Arrow Special

Unequal Britain

A Report on the Cycle of Inequality

by Frank Field

Has the Welfare State made British society more equal since the war?

Frank Field, Director of the Child Poverty Action Group, draws together evidence from all the major social reports to ask if there is a cycle of inequality in which a large number of people are trapped. The report examines

★ Whether all British children have an equal chance of surviving birth?
★ Does the education system make society more or less equal?
★ Have income differentials between rich and poor changed since the war?
★ Are income inequalities reflected in the work place?
★ Do the rich enjoy better health?
★ Do the poor have equal access to a decent home?
★ Is wealth becoming more evenly distributed?

Breaking Up

A Practical Guide to Separation, Divorce and Coping on
Your Own

by Rosemary Simon

No divorce is entirely free of worry and hardship. Difficult
questions concerning children, money and the family home
have to be resolved—as well as the daunting problems of
coping on your own and the painful business of picking
up the pieces and starting life afresh.

★ How do you get a separation or divorce?
★ What are your rights to the family home?
★ Do you qualify for legal aid?
★ What should you know about maintenance?
★ Who can assist if you are short of money?
★ How can you find accommodation?
★ What about your children?
★ Where can you meet new friends?
★ What are the challenges of a second marriage?
★ Whom can you turn to for help with problems?

This book provides the answers to these and many other
critical questions.